Cheetham's passion...carries the reader into an ever-deepening appreciation of the huge importance of Henry Corbin for the reevaluation of vision and imagination.
–James Hillman

IMAGINAL LOVE

The Meanings of Imagination
in Henry Corbin and James Hillman

TOM CHEETHAM

SPRING PUBLICATIONS
THOMPSON, CONN.

Published by Spring Publications, Inc.
Thompson, Conn.
www.springpublications.com

First Edition 2015

ISBN: 978-0-88214-032-2

Library of Congress Control Number: 2015934978

The paper used in this publication meets the minimum requirements of
the American National Standard for Information Sciences – Permanence
of Paper for Printed Library Materials, ANSI Z39.48-1992

CONTENTS

To the memory of James Hillman.
A good friend who I never met.

Preface

These chapters present some implications of a vision that places the imagination at the center of reality. It continues a long conversation I have been having with myself and many others and is the fruit of a twenty-five year engagement with the works of C.G. Jung, Henry Corbin, and James Hillman. It stands perfectly well on its on its own I think, but for those who have read any of my earlier books, the themes will have special resonance as I have discussed them before from different points of view and in several different contexts. Language is a central theme of this book and of Corbin's "psycho-cosmology" that provides its orientation. For a reader new to the material, Chapter 1 provides my most recent attempt to introduce Corbin's thought and his vision of imagination to a general audience. A more detailed treatment of his life and work can be found in *The World Turned Inside Out: Henry Corbin and Islamic Mysticism* (Woodstock, Conn.: Spring Journal Inc., 2003).

I am deeply grateful to Catherine Baumgartner for helping to arrange a truly wonderful long weekend in the Bay area in April 2013. Richard Stein of the Jung Institute of San Francisco and Laurel McCabe of Sonoma State University's program in depth psychology were wonderful hosts, and the audiences for my four talks were among the best I have ever had. My thanks to everyone who was there and to all those who worked hard to organize the events. Many thanks to Michael Lerner of Commonweal for excellent conversations and penetrating questions. A recording of our conversation at Sonoma State is available online through the New School at Commonweal.

A special note of continuing thanks to Susan Cooper for her enthusiasm and encouragement and for being my best and most useful reader.

Earlier versions of Chapters 1 and 4 were presented at the C.G. Jung Institute of San Francisco, 12 April 2013.

Some sections of Chapter 2 were presented as part of the lecture "The Ocean in Which We Live: Language and Imagination in Corbin, Jung & Hillman" at the C.G. Jung Center for Studies in Analytical Psychology, Brunswick, Maine, 12 November 2011.

Versions of Chapter 3 were presented at Sonoma State University, 11 April 2013 and at the C.G. Jung Center for Studies in Analytical Psychology, Brunswick, Maine, 22 April 2012.

Chapter 5 was presented at the C.G. Jung Center for Studies in Analytical Psychology, Brunswick, Maine, 8 June 2013.

Versions of Chapter 6 formed the bases for a day-long workshop for the Jung Society of Utah in Salt Lake City, 16 November, 2013, and a presentation at the Celebration of the work of James Hillman at the Dallas Institute of Humanities and Culture, 7 December 2013.

1

Your Autonomy Is a Fiction

It has been over twenty years since I first heard of Henry Corbin and read his book on Ibn 'Arabī. I had no idea I would spend so long in his company. My feelings about his work have been complicated. At the beginning, my generally mystified delight was sporadically and rudely punctuated by something like scorn, bordering even on repulsion. I had the good fortune to begin with his most accessible and perhaps finest book, *Creative Imagination in the Sufism of Ibn 'Arabī*. It makes serious demands on the reader, but it is a beautiful and even thrilling work of genius. My attraction to the book was for a long time mingled with a deep puzzlement about what he was doing. I could not *place* him. The volume is not a scholarly treatise. It isn't history. It isn't a study of myth. It isn't psychology. It isn't philosophy. I had never read any theology, and so I didn't know it when I first read it, but it isn't really that either. I have gradually come to see that it is in fact all of these things and more. Engaging with Henry Corbin can be a very disorienting and unsettling experience. His best work violates the norms of any discipline, any category you try to fit it in, and draws you into a strange and unstable world where the imagination reigns supreme. This explains the fascination I felt right from the first pages of the book. The repulsion that I sometimes felt came from the preconceptions I had about Christianity and the monotheistic tradition as a whole. I was raised in a secular home, and my very liberal education gave me every reason to feel nothing but disdain for and suspicion of the entirely patriarchal and authoritarian religions that I was quite sure Judaism, Christianity, and Islam essentially are. And yet for Corbin, the Holy Books provide access to worlds of wonder, beauty, truth, and love far beyond the powers of a merely human imagination. When I was under his spell, this seemed entirely natural and quite wonderful, but sometimes the secular rationalist in me would startle awake and recoil in horror. That doesn't happen to me anymore.

How are we to read Corbin? His writing is complex, subtle, difficult, eclectic, and often simultaneously beautiful and obscure. He was in easy command of at least half a dozen languages as well as the histories of philosophy and theology in several cultures, ancient and modern, Eastern and Western. The scholarly literature on his work provides a number of critiques by academics who insist on seeing him only as a fellow scholar and historian, and some of them have not been kind in their assessments. But to understand him and the nature of the world he invites us to enter we need to recognize the real nature of his life's work. Henry Corbin was above all else a master of Fiction. In what follows I will try to explain what I mean by that. It is important for each of us as individuals, and together as participants in a common world now illuminated day and night by the detonations of literalist fundamentalisms north and south, east and west, left, right, and center.

It is perhaps the chief merit of Corbin that he can help us, in his own words, to "transmute idols into icons" and so defuse the destructive power of literalism and fundamentalism at the heart, in the imagination. To anticipate: Corbin was a master of the visionary recital, the dramatic narrative, and if we understand what this truly means then we will come to see that Fiction in this great sense is the repository of all knowledge, and all truth. Literal truth is always false.

Poets and artists know this, as do the most creative of those in more seemingly literal pursuits. The poet Robert Duncan spoke of "fictive certainties" and James Hillman explained depth psychology to us through the notion of "healing fictions." It is hard to entirely dispel the common-sense idea that fiction is the opposite of truth. In reality, fiction is the only possible means of expressing the truth, and it is the ultimate praise to call Corbin a master dramatist.

I want to provide something of an overview of Corbin's life and thought, but I am not going to present a dispassionate and scholarly account of the "complete Henry Corbin." First of all, his work is too vast and complex for that. But also I find myself no longer interested in an "objective" reading of his work. If you are drawn into his world as I was, it changes you. Initially I tried to get my bearings by determining where he was standing, and so in my first book, and here and there in the others, I have tried to be more or less detached and to give an accurate account of what Corbin thought and believed and how he imagined. But over the years it has mattered less and less to me whether I was getting Corbin "right" and more and more whether I was getting me right. Now I find it very hard to draw clear distinctions between us and frankly I don't care quite so much whether Corbin would like what I am doing with his work or not. I found it held me back if I had to keep looking over my shoulder to see if he approved. So increasingly I pedal on my own. But I think this is really part of what he intended. Because, as with Jung, one of the virtues of reading Corbin is that his work leads you towards yourself. It is probably also important to say at the outset that there are really three major influences at work in my remarks, as will become clear. Henry Corbin, of course, and also Jung, whose work I know a bit about, but also, and crucially, James Hillman. It used to surprise me that in many audiences of Jungians that I have spoken to there have been few if any readers of Hillman. In my imagination, Jung and Hillman are entirely entwined, as I read them side by side or in alternating succession for many years. I doubt there is much in anything I have written that can't be found in Corbin, Jung, or Hillman. That's fine with me—I think that a life's work devoted to making their ideas more widely known is worthwhile.

The First and Final Fact

Over the years I have reworked themes from Corbin's writings several times over. I say this without apology. I have done it because the material is dauntingly complex, endlessly rich, and strangely elusive. Corbin's great vision is an extremely densely woven multidimensional fabric and the patterns become clearer the more of it you can keep in sight at once. Describing it is hard because you can only follow one thread at a time. Each time I do I see some new pattern. At its best, this repetition is a kind of alchemical process. It is particularly apt that the words I want to use to describe the content of Corbin's writings include "material" and "subject matter." There is nothing abstract in his work, though often his vocabulary is philosophical and obscure to many readers. The matters he deals with demand to be worked again and again, and every time they reveal new meanings and evoke new surprises. I love it. There is no end to the grand drama of interpreting Corbin. There is of course a kind of learning that proceeds in another way—we answer questions and solve problems, figure out how to do things that transform the world for better or often, worse, and then we move on to new questions.

It's very exciting. This energy drives the modern world. But with psychological and spiritual matters it is different. The questions are never answered, the issues never resolved, the depth and significance never exhausted.

So let me try once again to follow a path that leads into the world Corbin invites us to enter. He likes to talk about "cosmology" and "cosmogony" and this kind of language sometimes puts people off. But we will indeed be outlining a cosmology, a great vision of reality. It is one that requires a good deal from us if we are to understand him: it requires that we imagine very differently than many in the modern world are used to doing. Let's plunge right in and start with the theology. This will be highly compressed, but I think you will get the gist of it in any case. One obstacle may be that some people are uncomfortable with theology, as I was for most of my life, and have lots of resistances to theological talk. If you are one of them I want you to try to suppress your aversion. This is theology properly done – it's not Dogmatics and Church Doctrine but rather a style of imagining. Think psychologically – for we need to *imagine* our way into this realm. This is not science, and we are not trying to discover facts and natural laws or abstract truths. The criteria for recognizing truth in these matters are not those of natural science, but this cosmological investigation does require its own pragmatism – a spiritual pragmatism. Our question should be: "What does it do to you if you imagine yourself and the world this way?"

To begin: the Person is the first and final reality – the alpha and the omega. There is nothing more fundamental. No human being can be entirely explained by physics, biology, sociology, or history. The person is an irreducible mystery, more basic than matter or energy, time or space, and like these, indefinable. Corbin is a theologian in the

Abrahamic tradition, and the ultimate Real, the active and living source of reality, is a personal God. But we have to banish any thought of the figures on the ceiling of the Sistine Chapel. This God is not Michelangelo's Old Man with a Beard. Don't think "person" in a finite human sense. If you do, the hierarchical and sexist image of God the Father will stop you dead in your tracks and you won't see what is going on here at all. God, as the archetypal, ultimate Person is not a thing. We are things, of a sort, but not as persons. A person is not a thing. As finite, created beings we have lots of thing-ness about us, but God doesn't. We do because as the distance from God increases, so does the opacity of beings, their density and darkness. They become less luminous, less alive, more like "objects" and less like "subjects," less like persons.

God is not a "being" at all, not even an infinite one. God is Be-ing in the sense that without God, nothing can be. The "being" of God is verbal and transitive – the being of God makes everything else be. God says "Be!" and things spring into existence. We are swimming in the waters of Creation all the time. We breathe the winds that blow upon the face of the deep. We are "con-spiritors" with God, breathing in the Breath of the Compassionate. And this cosmos of created being is not just a bunch of vaguely defined "stuff" out of which identifiable things somehow develop. As God is the ground of all being, so God is the ground of the "eachness" of things, the uniqueness and particularity of the things of the world. As with God's "being," so God is One in a verbal sense – God is the active source of the individuality of things. God "unifies," makes each being unique, makes each of us who we are – makes each of us able to say "I." In the absence of the "unification" of the divine, there can be no individuality, no *individuation*. So God is the ground and source of our being *and* our individuality.

There is a profound corollary to this. If God is not a being, then *belief* in God is simply not an issue. To ask "do you believe in God?" is like asking "do you believe in Santa Claus, the Loch Ness monster, the Higgs boson, or global warming?" In all these cases there is some "thing" the existence of which is at issue and we could do some research and find out what the truth is. "Believing" is part of a world system that gives rise to the modern scientific attitude towards reality. Believing is a transitional state. It is something you do only until you *know*. And in the case of belief in the existence of God, it is generally mingled with doubt, which when unacknowledged gives rise to anxiety and so eventually to rigidity and belligerence. That is not what is going on in Corbin's cosmology. We can escape from the narrow confines of believing and knowing. There is a far larger and more inclusive form of life in which believing and knowing themselves have useful and rightful places. That freer, more comprehensive and more natural stance towards reality is based on Imagination. All questions about God are properly matters of imagination.

God is not a being that can be known, but rather should be re-visioned as the open field of imagination itself. This is completely natural and unremarkable when we imagine ourselves and reality in the right way. What way? What style of imagination is Corbin revealing to us? How are we to imagine? To experience Corbin's vision, we have to imagine Reality as *open*. The fundamental metaphors become *openness* and *light*. Corbin speaks of a Gothic style of cosmology, calling to mind the luminous polychrome glories and vast upward thrust of the great cathedrals of Europe. In such a cosmos, the Person must be the first and final reality. For not only is Personhood an open category – it is *the* open category, the archetype of openness.

And now the rest of Corbin's major themes start rushing in. If we first move into this larger world where imagination is the central fact of life, then it is easier to understand what he means by "the angelic function of beings." All beings are potential windows onto a divine and endless landscape. That is their Face of Light, their connection to the Divine. But since no being is the endless Open, the unlimited Light, every being must also have a Dark Face, an opacity and finite darkness. When we see only this dark Face, we see beings as "objects," not as subjects, and they seem lifeless and abstract. These are the objects of believing and knowing, the objects of science and of the rationality of engineering. The angelic function of beings is their capacity to serve as subjects, as *icons,* gateways into the divine. In this sense every being has an Angel. The Angel is the immediate source of the personal face of every being. For anything whatever to be *present,* it has to be present to *someone* and it has to be regarded, looked at, in a mutual, personal relation. Otherwise, at the outer limit of Creation, there can only be abstract objects which are not looked at by anyone. And then they disappear. Presence and personhood are complementary terms. You can't have one without the other. That beings can be experienced at all requires that they be *present* to us, and us to them. "God" is the possibility of that mutual, personal Presence. So God is the opened field of the imagination where the mutual presence of persons and things can occur. Person, Presence, and Imagination are the three interpenetrating attributes of the God beyond Being that Corbin reveals to us.

The persons to whom beings are present in the first instance are the angels – the angels of their being. We all have an angel. Every being has an angel. This is necessary because God-beyond-Being cannot be known and cannot be encountered. The mysterious depths of that ultimate principle remain forever beyond our imagination and beyond encounter since that God provides the possibility of all imagination and encounter. What we *can have* and what we *do get,* are angels – absolutely essential intermediaries between Creation and the Ultimate Enigma. The faces of angels are really all we can ever imagine of the divinity beyond. Angels are created beings and so have a Dark Face and a Light Face, and it is the Dark Faces that we see – though they look intensely illuminated from where we stand. It is a matter of degree, and there are numberless degrees of "angelicity" in the grand hierarchy of angels. The endless depths and heights of the world the angels inhabit is guaranteed by the wonderful fact that every angel in turn has its own angel. The function of the angel is always to reveal depth and serve as a luminous icon that stands as Light to the relative Dark of whatever stage a being has attained. The potential for motion onwards is unending – motion both higher and deeper, for here they are the same. This is the function of the angel as the "Angel Out Ahead." In the imagination of this cosmology, even the Supreme Being, the "God" of common theology, has an Angel Out Ahead to guarantee the endless Openness of reality.

It is natural to misinterpret this whole scheme and see it "upside down." This is the result of a reading of Plato that has gotten hold of the Western religious imagination. It results in some profound misunderstandings. The movement of transcendence, which is another name for the angelic dynamic we are talking about, is not "upwards" towards a disembodied realm of vaporous abstraction and vaguely "spiritual" purity. A standard reading of Plato's metaphysics has it that the Forms or Ideas are like intellectual categories—abstract, bodiless universals that exist in some realm of the mind. This is completely at odds with the basic thrust of the Abrahamic cosmology we are grappling with here, which is profoundly sensuous, embodied, and personal. Corbin wants to blame this wrong turn in Western thought and culture, in its early stages at least, on Aristotle who, Corbin says, interpreted the Platonic forms not as personified principles, as he should have done, but rather as abstract intellectual categories. Corbin pointedly says that the Aristotelian "logical universal" is nothing more than the dead body of an Angel. Corbin's spiritual master, the twelfth-century Persian mystic Suhrawardi, did indeed interpret Plato's world of ideal Forms in terms of a Zoroastrian cosmology replete with angels. This was his way of reconciling Platonism with Islam. The angels assure that the Person is a fundamental category—they populate a thoroughly personified cosmos. A more "Jungian" reading of Plato in which the Forms are regarded as Archetypes and are given an explicitly psychological meaning is much closer to what Corbin thinks the monotheistic tradition should do, and often did do with Plato.

In the Christian tradition personal resurrection at the end of time is supposed to be *bodily* resurrection. This may seem a bit ridiculous if you are limited to literalist materialism. But how should sensuous, personal, and embodied transcendence be imagined? The notion of embodiment has to be revisioned in accord with the central place of imagination in this cosmology. Corbin speaks of subtle, spiritual bodies that are more, not less, real than the dense and opaque bodies we know. And of course there is an endless progression of degrees of embodied reality. It is a matter of degrees of being—of degrees of intensity of being. As the

Angel Out Ahead leads you onwards, you get more real, more concrete, and more individual.

If we take our stand with Corbin, the person is the first and final fact. Everything is personified, everything is personal. Not subjective and personal but entirely objective and personal. Not personal in the sense that everything refers to *me*. Corbin asks: What would a world without a Face, that is to say, without a "look" be? It would not *be* at all. An impersonal reality is utterly inconceivable. The materialist fantasy whereby reality is made up of matter and energy, aggregated in suitably complex arrangements that eventually give rise to life and consciousness and human beings is well embedded in the modern scientific imagination, but it makes no sense. Such a world is senseless in the same way that it is Faceless. It can have no *look*. To exist a being must be Present. And Presence is the fundamental attribute of the Person. This is why there must be Angels. They are the Faces of the inaccessible God. They guarantee the particularity and the concrete reality of the world.

The Literal and the Imaginal

If you followed that, at least in spirit if not in detail, then you may have fallen under Corbin's spell. People do. It is a marvelous vision, and of course it is not Corbin's alone. But the more enthusiastic you become the more careful you have to be not to take it literally. This grand cosmology provides a mode of imagining and the contours of a form of life. It does not provide truth or certainty or dogma. Quite the opposite. It opens the mind and frees the imagination. It lets in the Breath of the Compassionate, and if you are very lucky, "graced" I would say, it helps to open your heart. It is the story of an open cosmos, not a closed one. So the Truth it contains is incomplete, unfinished, in process. It is a Telling, a story, a great and wonderful drama that contains us. We are living it, creating it as we live. Or we may choose to deny it, by claiming to have the Truth about Reality. Then we fall away from our charge to become persons, and we risk becoming objects rather than subjects and we stop being "con-spiritors" in this grand, breathing Speech. Take all this wonderful business about Angels – if you try to understand the angels "literally," which I suppose means as beautiful, invariably feminine, human-like figures with wings, then what you will end up with is an object – just the opposite of an angel. You will have exactly, and tragically, only the dead body of an angel.

Here is a story that may help to explain. It is the tale of a tension between Corbin and James Hillman. And also, I think, of a tension in Corbin's work – between the young radical and his later more conservative stance. The two were colleagues at the Eranos Conferences in Ascona. Hillman lectured at Eranos almost every year from 1966 to 1979, the year after Corbin's death. Corbin was at first quite enthusiastic about what he saw as a "rebirth of the gods" in Hillman's work. But in the preface to the second edition of *Spiritual Body and Celestial Earth,* written in March 1978, seven months before his death, he voiced some serious reservations. He thought the increasingly widespread use of the term *imaginal* was bound to lead to confusion and error. He had introduced the Latin term *mundus imaginalis* to refer to the world of the Imagination as it appears in the works of Suhrawardi and Ibn 'Arabī and their followers. This is the Imaginal world – the realm of the angels and of all the phenomena of religious experience. It is not the product of human imagination, which is a lesser and derivative manifestation. From one point of view, everything is Imagination since everything derives from the creative acts of God. But from another, there is a gulf between merely human imagining, from which monstrous images and evil acts may derive, and the higher world of the angelic beings who appear in the visions of the mystics and the prophets. Corbin was upset that Hillman and others were co-opting his terminology and applying it outside of the "precisely defined schema" provided by the masters of Iranian Islam. And so indeed they were. Some have used Corbin's terminology in an explicitly religious context, but Hillman's lifework has been, I think wrongly, understood as exactly the "secularization of the imaginal" that Corbin feared. Hillman famously railed against the contemporary quest for the "spiritual" and argued for the central importance of "soul," *anima,* rather than "spirit." Circling around this conflict are many of the quandaries that I find most compelling and difficult.

Neither Corbin nor Hillman were systematic thinkers. Both ranged freely across academic and disciplinary boundaries, and the range and scope of the writings of each are vast. Hillman owes an enormous debt to Corbin. Their work overlaps in many fundamental respects, and so no easy comparison is possible. Still, it may be useful to try to specify the nature of the disagreement that caused the rupture between them. Corbin was a mystic and a heretic and a radical boundary breaker within the Abrahamic tradition. As such he was able to straddle the boundaries that separate the great monotheisms and provide us with a synoptic view such as no one within the tradition had ever done. He took a cue from Suhrawardi's reconciliation of Zoroastrianism and Islam and showed us what the prophetic tradition looks like more-or-less as a whole, from Abraham to Mohammed, and beyond. He sketched the outlines of a post-Islamic Christianity based on the eternal and immediate presence of the Holy Spirit. He was a brilliant and unique Protestant Christian theologian and a stood passionately *within* the prophetic tradition. In his mystic vision, the supreme act of the creative Imagination is prayer, and the supreme value is the inner Temple in each of us, as both Sanctuary and Gate.

As a young man Corbin didn't hesitate to adapt the rallying cry of the Marxists and proclaim "Heretics of the world unite!" Throughout his life he was attracted by the marginal figures in all religions. He always routinely and enthusiastically ignored the boundaries of acceptable faith and practice set by orthodox dogma. And yet he was clearly alarmed by Hillman's adaptation of his work. This startlingly eclectic supporter of heretics everywhere stood firm against what he doubtless perceived as a violation of the sacred. While deeply disdainful of institutional religion, he was a fervent and powerful advocate for the reality of the Temple. The problem with organized religion is that it invariably tries to make the Temple a public monument, when in fact it can only appear in the deep interior of an individual. That is the true location of the sacred precinct, the boundaries of which must be kept inviolate. The deep interiority and objective reality of the Temple is the most important thing for Corbin. Like the Holy Grail it is difficult to access, and like the Grail Castle not just anyone can enter. It would, he thought, be a mistake with fatal consequences to confuse the imaginal realm in which the Temple exists with the chaotic jumble that is the normal state of the human psyche.

James Hillman was a psychologist first and foremost, and no theologian. He was always the mercurial Trickster. He was suspicious of enclosures and fixed boundaries and so could not comfortably enter Corbin's Temple, or stay there for long. He wanted the Gate but feared the Wall. He was suspicious of anything fixed and permanent. And he simply did not share Corbin's feeling for a hierarchical cosmos. For Corbin prayer is not a request for anything but the expression, as he says, of a mode of being–one which is open to mystery. But Corbin's imagination and his prayer are directed vertically. Corbin is always seeing into another world, transcendent to this one. For him, imagination is *sublimation*. Hillman's imagination is intensely this-worldly, and profoundly *concrete* in a sense I will make clear shortly. He expands on certain themes in Corbin's work that Corbin himself was ill-equipped to develop. Hillman's practice is about the imagining soul as a *process* and about *undoing* things. In this he shared Corbin's hatred of idolatry and fundamentalism. But his imagination does not move vertically, as Corbin's always does. He was fond of a phrase from Plotinus: "the motion of the soul is circular," and he distrusted the otherworldly drive of the "spiritual" that animates so much of Corbin's work. Hillman says that the mode of imagining of the Spirit is literalism. Science, philosophy, and theology have traditionally been spiritual disciplines in this sense, and have tended to strive for a stable and universally valid Truth. Corbin is spiritual to the core and yet he is no literalist idolator and helps us to see how we might be spiritual without constantly falling into idolatry. He is teller of stories, and a destroyer of idols *par excellence*. And yet in his late attempt to control the interpretation of the meaning of the "imaginal" he shows traces of the very rigidity he spent his life combatting.

People are complex and unsystematic beings and I happily admit that I need both Corbin and Hillman in my life. Corbin gave me access to the Temple when I could not have lived without it. He also made it possible for me to feel a connection to the beauty of a tradition that is my cultural heritage. But James Hillman too saved my life. I found his work first, when I desperately needed it. Through him I discovered Corbin. Hillman not only made me aware of Corbin but made it possible for me to move into Corbin's world. It was Hillman's work that perhaps paradoxically helped me overcome the scorn I felt for the tradition Corbin represents. Hillman's vision gives us freedom. He gives us permission. We all need permission to find the things we most desire. I remember a classroom incident from years ago. I was reading Hillman's *Re-Visioning Psychology* with a small class of undergraduate women who were a joy to work with. I don't remember what the exact occasion was, but one day we were doing a close analysis of a chapter in that wonderful book, six of us sitting around the small table teasing out the meaning of some passage, and suddenly one of the best and most intense students slapped both hands on the table with a cry of delight and exclaimed: "Oh my God! You mean you can *think* that?!" That remains the most memorable moment of my teaching career. Hillman had just that effect on me when I first read him – his idiosyncratic vision of Jung's psychology was what I had been looking for all my life. I am still smitten.

What may be Hillman's central insight derives directly from Corbin. It is his account of the difference between the literal and the imaginal. To understand it, begin with Corbin's distinction between the idol and the icon, on which hangs his entire psycho-cosmology. The goal of incarnate life is to be in love with the world. Such a life "in sympathy with beings" is lived in love. But, Corbin warns us, this can go off wrong in two ways. You can love a being without perceiving its transcendence – then you experience it as opaque, static, and fixed. Then it becomes an idol, and you become an idolator, a fundamentalist. Or, you can be so in love with transcendence itself that you ignore the present reality of the being through whom the transcendence must be manifested. Then the icon loses its grounding in the world. This is the trap of a disembodied Spirituality that attempts to transcend the world without ever living in it. Both of these mistakes occur with distressing regularity in the lives, and especially in the love lives of all of us. The first, when we mistake lust for love, and turn the Lover into an object; the second, when we are so dumbstruck by the aura of the Angel manifesting in a human being that we cannot see the concrete person through whom She shines. In both cases Corbin tells us, we become incapable of real sympathy for the beings among whom we move and breathe.

Real sympathy for the world, incarnate sympathy, requires a perpetual dance, a rhythmic call, and response between you and the others who share your world. It is a "con-spiracy," and mutual breathing in and out. In the Islamic doctrine of perpetual creation that Corbin relies on every being is at each instant simultaneously descending to earth and ascending to Heaven, and the friction this creates provides the light and the energy to keep all of Creation in existence. Idolatry is the futile and destructive attempt to grind it all to a halt and plunge us into darkness by severing the connection between transcendence and immanence, between the present moment and the eternal. This happens whether your idols are made of the literal dead matter of modernist science, or the disembodied Spirits of a distant Heaven.

In my reading, Corbin's chief fault lies in his relentless upward flight towards transcendence. He was, by all accounts, and by the evidence of his work, a mystic, with a remarkable ability to see into the beyond. This has its virtues, and I love his work. But most of us are not, and should not try to be mystics. We live here. Corbin helps us to see how to do that. But his vision needs grounding, and I find that in Hillman's work, strange as that may seem to some. Hillman is grounded by his insistence on the primacy of soul, and by his profound understanding of alchemy. He understands Corbin's distinction between the idol and the icon as the source of energy and motion that it is, without flying off into Heaven in search of an abstract Angel. Hillman grounds Corbin's work by driving home the distinction between the literal and the imaginal, and explaining to us that the literal is not to be confused with the *concrete*. Any reality supposed to be literal: *this* fact, *this* rock, this Book, this Truth, anything we try to pin down as stable, universal and immutable—the rock-solid facts of existence—these are all *abstractions*. The literal is always abstract—because reality is so much more than we can ever know or experience or imagine. Nothing stays put—everything real, embodied, *concrete,* ramifies, multiplies, sends out roots and shoots and explodes into images. There is no end to telling the stories of persons and things. *Only the fictive is concrete.* That is why there is no end to the telling of stories. Of people, of things. Fiction, myths, fairy tales, gossip and rumors—these are the fictions of persons. The astounding richness of the stories science tells us, and continues to tell us seemingly without end—these are some of the fictions of *things.* Nothing stays put.

And this is why belief is such a dangerous thing. Belief is to the literal as imagination is to the fictive. Belief wants to *know;* the imagination wants to hear more stories, to unfold the endless tale of reality. And so the primary mode of *being* for humans has got to be Listening. Not "I think, therefore I am," but rather "I listen, therefore I am." Pay attention and listen to the beings you love. Hear what they are telling you. Let the Angel act on you, through them – they will open you.

For the Sake of the Images

Hillman's reading of Corbin is psychological. He was a therapist, not a theologian. His focus was on the sufferings, pathologies and psychic turmoil of everyday life. The primary text in which he makes clear his departure from Corbin is this:

> Clearly, pathologizings of the image do *not* belong to the *mundus imaginalis* as [Corbin] has given us this word. But in the soul-making of actual psychotherapy, pathologizings are often the *via regia* into the imaginal. The refinement of our imaginal sensibility must begin where sensibility itself begins. From the gross to the subtle is an operation, not an ontology. The ontological priority of Corbin's world is nonetheless arrived at via the operational priority of Jung's method – because we must begin where we have fallen, flat on our backs in personal pain. The difference between Jung and Corbin can be resolved if we practice Jung's technique with Corbin's vision, that is, active imagination is not for the sake of the doer and *our* actions in the sensible world of literal realities, but for the sake of the images and to where they can take us – *their* realization.[1]

---

1 "On the Necessity of Abnormal Psychology," in James Hillman, *Facing the Gods* (Dallas: Spring Publications, 1980), 33n5.

The "refinement of imaginal sensibility" is the challenge – that would be learning to listen, to attend to the fictive, the imaginal in our dreams and in our waking lives, which are so shot through with fragments of dream, image, story, gossip, and hearsay – the seeming junk and refuse and nonsense that makes up so much of our inner lives. If we ever stop long enough to attend to what is going on with our own psyche, our own incarnate reality, let alone in the psyches and bodies of others, all of us here know the kinds of depths we can find. But also Hillman says we need to practice Jung's method with Corbin's vision. To repeat: "active imagination... is for the sake of the images and where they can take us, *their* realization." Corbin teaches that it is not *your* individuation that is at stake, but that of the Angel. He wrote: "The active subject is in reality not you, your autonomy is a fiction. In reality, you are the subject of a verb in the passive (you are the *ego* of a *cogitor*)." But the *cogito*, the thought of an Angel, is in no way abstract – the best approximation we have is alchemy in the sense in which Corbin, Jung, and Hillman use the term. This thought incarnates, it embodies, it individuates. And as Corbin emphasizes, "Alchemy is the Sister of Prophecy." This kind of "thinking," which is movement in the imaginal world, is the fundamental action of the religious imagination. In Corbin's great cosmic drama, the challenge is to cooperate with the angel of your being – your celestial Twin – without whom you are lost in "vagabondage and perdition" but who, equally, needs *you* in order to be whole, to attain the full reality due to a person. Lacking all contact with that Angelic Presence we are bereft of the light and energy that animates, gives soul and living body to the world we make around ourselves by learning to *Be!* who we are destined to become. This drama gives meaning and direction to the story of individuation – it is not your story, or not yours alone. It is the story of the marriage of the two parts of your being – that is the grand adventure, the visionary recital that lies at the heart of Corbin's Great Work.

One crucial element missing in the tale of Corbin's world as I have been telling it is the absolutely central place that music has in his imagination. It is music, the harmony of things, that ties all creation together. In the Beginning the voices of the Angels sang the world into being. The Angel's voice often comes as music. It most often comes only as the fragment of a song that we almost hear, at the edge of the world we know, and even the dimmest memory of it can break your heart. If your autonomy is a fiction, then the goal of the alchemical work, the goal of individuation, is to learn that the real autonomy is to let go of what you think of as your self. You are a song being sung elsewhere, and resonating everywhere. Learn to let your drama unfold and follow the sound of the Angel, always just on the threshold of consciousness. Listen. Always listen for that faint song of the Angel whose Voice it takes more than a lifetime to learn to hear.

2

The Extensive Self

The Great Disjunction

Henry Corbin is hardly the only thinker to have proposed an alternative to the historicist account of the world that undergirds modern science and scholarship. I was lucky enough to know one such scholar, and his version of the story complements Corbin's approach, though in some respects it is radically different. Where Corbin is thoroughly ahistorical, this account is grounded in history, but allows for a far-reaching reassessment of the nature of Western consciousness, and makes the received account of the nature of history and time problematic at best.

In a startling and original interpretation of the development of Western societies, the historian F. Edward Cranz[1] argued that the transition from the "ancient" world to the "modern" depended upon an unacknowledged but profoundly important revolution in consciousness:

> The ancients – and by the ancients I mean the Greeks, the Romans, and the Graeco-Roman Christians – the ancients experienced an awareness open to what lay around them, and they experienced no sense of dichotomy between their

1 See my remembrance, "F. Edward Cranz-In Memoriam," *American Cusanus Society Newsletter,* Vol. XXVII, No. 1 (July 2010), 17-21.

awareness and everything else. What they found
in their own minds or intellects was of like charac-
ter with much of what was outside it; what they
found in the world could in large part move directly
into their minds and be possessed by it. There was
an *ontological continuity* between what happened
in their intellects and what happened in the cosmos or world.[2]

During the twelfth century in the Christian West, a fundamental reorientation of the ancient categories of thought
and the nature of experience itself occurred. Cranz gave a
summary statement of the "reorientation thesis" for his
colleagues in 1985:

> There was a general reorientation of categories
> of thought c. 1100 AD, say in the generation of
> Anselm and Abelard. Against the ancient posi-
> tion...in which sensation and intellection lead
> to conjunction and union with what was sensed
> or intellected, we find a dichotomy between the
> mind and what is outside it, between meanings
> and things. [Rather than the] ancient *extensive
> self*, a self open to the world around it, we find a
> move to an *intensive self*, a universe of mean-
> ings separated by a dichotomy from the world of
> things. Finally, against an ancient reason which
> is primarily a *vision* of what is, we find a move-
> ment toward a *reason* based on the systematic

2 F. Edward Cranz, "The Reorientation of Western Thought
c. 1100 AD: The Break with the Ancient Tradition and Its Consequences for Renaissance and Reformation," Delivered at the Duke
University Center for Medieval and Renaissance Studies, March 24,
1982 (personal manuscript; my italics).

coherence of what is said or thought. [These phases] are held together in the experience of what we call language.[3]

The ancient extensive self "was in the fullest sense part of a single realm of being and indeed, potentially identical with it." The kind of knowing that is open to this self, is in Cranz's terms, "conjunctive." The new categories of thought and being that characterize the intensive self include dichotomous, "disjunctive" forms of knowing. There appears a split between the knower and the known, and therefore a distinction between meanings and things. Language is constituted as a human system opposed to the "things themselves" that exist outside of human language. Knowledge, rather than being a result of union with what is the known becomes a result of a process of "reasoning" that depends upon coherence within language. Knowledge comes to "lack all immediacy." This twelfth-century reorientation is the foundation of the modern sense of a self alienated in the world and trapped in a system of merely human meanings.

Cranz said that our mode of thought "is different from, even alien to, all previous thought, and...there is nothing normative, or even normal, about it, or us."[4] But it is of course not just a change in modes of *thought* that he is concerned with, but rather ways of experiencing the world. He wrote: "The thrust of my argument is not that there were different theories about the same seeing and knowing, but rather that there were different seeings and

---

3 F. Edward Cranz, *Reorientations of Western Thought from Antiquity to the Renaissance,* ed. Nancy S. Struever (Aldershot, Hampshire: Ashgate, 2006), xii (my italics).

4 Cranz, "The Reorientation of Western Thought c. 1100AD."

knowings."[5] And he clearly thought that whatever we may have gained by this transition, something had been lost. His colleague and editor Nancy Struever tells us that Cranz's project in "phenomenological hermeneutics" is an attempt to reclaim an experience of the psyche that was consciously articulated by Aristotle. Struever says that Cranz's work

> shows... a deep sympathy with an Aristotelian psychology which presumes a continuum of capacities—sensation, perception, fantasy, memory, passions and intellect—that are continuously interactive... [He] describes a loss that transpires in the domain of experience: the post-Anselmian disjunction is a psychological deficit, a loss of "dimensionality." And the loss is our loss as well.[6]

Cranz was cautious and somewhat reticent about his thesis that the "ancients" experienced the world in a way radically different from ours. He knew he faced an uphill battle making his case. Struever comments that he "expressed many times his rueful awareness of the generally disbelieving scholarly response."[7] Although he often said that it shouldn't be possible to recapture this vanished way of knowing, he was living proof that it could be done. He said to me once that as he sat lost in contemplation over those ancient texts, sometimes he was afraid that he wouldn't be able to get back.

Another remarkable exercise in the phenomenological hermeneutics of medieval texts provides support for Cranz's thesis, and for the crucial importance of the twelfth century in the history of Western consciousness.

---

5 Cranz, *Reorientations of Western Thought*, xi.

6 Cranz, *Reorientations of Western Thought*, xi, xiv.

7 Ibid., xiv.

At issue for Ivan Illich in his study of Hugh of St. Victor (1096-1141) is the experience of reading, the hermeneutic *act* itself. Whereas Cranz's attention is on a revolution in the basic experience of the self and the world and with how knowledge was conceived, Illich is explicitly concerned with the experience of *reading*. He shows that during the twelfth century in the Latin West a transition occurred from one kind of "reading," one kind of hermeneutical situation, to another. As in Cranz's analysis, this is correlated with a change in the experience of the self and the nature of the act of knowing–in this case the knowledge acquired by reading. Illich sees Hugh as representative of the monastic approach to the Holy Book. He writes, "Reading, as Hugh perceives and interprets it, is an *ontologically remedial technique*."[8] It "is a remedy because it brings light back into a world from which sin banned it."[9] In the world of monastic readers, huddled over their parchment texts and reading aloud to themselves, the study of a text was an embodied activity, a challenge to the student's "heart and senses even more than to his stamina and brains."[10] "Study" meant something more akin to "sympathy" than to the abstract intellectual pursuit that it was to become, and the enlightenment that is the end result of this study is not the light of Reason as modern rationalists understand it. "The light of which Hugh speaks here brings man to a glow." Wisdom could shine through the pages of the Book, bringing the letters and symbols to light, "and kindle

---

8 Ivan Illich, *In the Vineyard of the Text: A Commentary to Hugh's Didascalicon* (Chicago: The University of Chicago Press, 1993), 11 (my italics).

9 Ibid., 20.

10 Ibid., 14.

the eye of the reader."[11] Wisdom is not only in the heart, but *in the Book itself,* as it is perceived with sympathy. Such sympathy is a form of the "conjunctive" knowing that was on the verge of disappearing even as Hugh was writing and reading. Perhaps Hugh is on the cusp already – the remedy is felt to be necessary not only because the world is Fallen, but because the conjunction is no longer occurring as a result of the "reading" of the manifold beings of Creation, but is already restricted to the literal, literary reading of the Word in Scripture.

For Henry Corbin the twelfth century also marks a turning point in Western consciousness, and a loss of sympathy with the beings of the world. The metaphysical, and phenomenological and hermeneutic catastrophe of the West is signaled, for Corbin, by the triumph of the Aristotelianism of Averroes over the Platonism of Avicenna with its Neoplatonic hierarchies of Angels. The catastrophe is the loss of contact with the worlds of the Angels. Corbin was a Platonist, and his theory of knowledge is "illuminationist." All knowledge comes from above by means of a vision of, or union with the archetypes, the Platonic Forms. The "giver of Forms" is the Angel. The *intellectus agens,* or Active Intelligence of medieval theology, is identified with the Angel Gabriel. He is the Angel of Humanity, and is *both* the Angel of Revelation and the Angel of Knowledge. Knowledge, whether granted freely via Revelation or gained with the cooperation of human intellect, is a result of illumination from above, not the culmination of a process of abstraction, deduction, or induction from the "data" of sense perception. And it is a result of "union" with the Forms which are known. Corbin would agree precisely with Cranz that

---

11 Ibid., 17-18.

in this kind of knowing "there [is] an ontological continuity between what happens in the intellect and what happens in the kosmos or world." Illuminationist epistemology depends upon what Cranz calls "conjunctive" knowing. And equally clearly, illuminative knowing is "ontologically remedial" precisely because as Illich says, the light of this knowledge "brings man to a glow." It raises us up from the world of darkness into which we have fallen.

The *extensive self* that Cranz, Illich, and Corbin describe in their very different ways reveals a primary human potential that each of them believed had been largely or completely lost in the modern West. As historians sensitive to how deeply we are embedded in our time and culture, Cranz and Illich both seem to have despaired of any return to such an expanded experience of the world. The great merit of Henry Corbin's work is that he provides us with a means of return – a method for escaping the alienated, isolated modern ego. He provides us with a method for re-establishing the ontological continuity between the human soul, the *anima humana,* and the soul of the world, the *anima mundi.* For Corbin, Platonist and mystic, we are not trapped in history – history is in us. The key unlocking the mysteries of illuminationist hermeneutics, that is to say, true spiritual hermeneutics, is the Imagination. The world of the Angel of Knowledge and of Revelation is the world of Imagination. The active Imagination is the foundation upon which the Active Intelligence, and therefore all knowledge, depends.

But in the history of Western thought after the disaster of the twelfth century, the Imagination as a source of knowledge has been almost entirely ignored. In the philosophies of the West, he writes, between the sense perceptions and the intuitions or categories of the intellect there has remained a void. That which ought to have taken its place between the two, and which in other times and places did occupy this intermediate space, that is to say the Active Imagination, has been left to the poets. The very thing that a rational and reasonable scientific philosophy cannot envisage is that the Active Imagination in man (one ought to say rather "agent imagination" in the way that medieval philosophy spoke of "intellectus agens") should have its own noetic or cognitive function, that is to say it gives us access to a region of Being which without that function remains closed and forbidden to us.[12]

For Corbin the human imagination is distinct from but continuous with the divine Imagination. It is our connection to the Angels and to God. And, he says, it has been left to the poets. It is in poetry and the arts that we will most readily come face to face with that creative imagination which is the life blood of the extensive self, of the human soul and the soul of the world. It is this creative activity that binds together body and mind, thought and being, the soul and the world.

Corbin's colleague C.G. Jung came to the same conclusion from a psychological rather than a theological starting point. Early in his seminal discussion of the "problem of types" he resolves the tensions between those opposites which have so vexed Western philosophy. His solution

---

12 Henry Corbin, *Spiritual Body and Celestial Earth: From Mazdean Iran to Shi'ite Iran,* trans. Nancy Pearson (Princeton, N.J.: Princeton University Press, 1989), vii.

is the same as Corbin's – he points to Imagination as a third and mediating factor. Thought and thing, mind and body, soul and world come together in the living processes of the psyche. *Esse in intellectu* and *esse in re* can only come together in *esse in anima*. Of the active life of the psyche he writes:

> This autonomous activity of the psyche, which can be explained neither as a reflex action to sensory stimuli nor as the executive organ of eternal ideas, is, like every vital process, a continually creative act. The psyche creates reality every day. The only expression I can use for this activity is fantasy... There is no psychic function that, through fantasy, is not bound up with the other psychic functions... Fantasy...seems to me to be the clearest expression of the specific activity of the psyche...it is the mother of all possibilities.[13]

Recall Streuver's claim that Cranz's *extensive self* has deep affinities with "an Aristotelian psychology which presumes a continuum of capacities – sensation, perception, fantasy, memory, passions and intellect – that are continuously inter-active."[14] What we find in the Platonism of Corbin and the psychological phenomenology of Jung is a psychology in which the continuous interaction of the faculties is made possible by imagination, which is regarded as the reigning power of the soul. The very lifeblood providing the coherence of the personality and binding together the soul and the world is "fantasy" – the creative and active

---

13 C.G. Jung, *Psychological Types,* Collected Works of C.G. Jung, trans. R.F.C. Hull, vol. 6 (Princeton, N.J.: Princeton University Press, 1976), par. 78.

14 Cranz, *Reorientations of Western Thought,* xi.

Imagination. It is the exercise of this faculty, conceived not as a merely human attribute but as continuous with the creative power of the world, that provides the means by which the intensive self can escape from its prison and enter that wider, more-than-human world.

The Ocean in Which We Live

Years ago I was a student of F. Edward Cranz. His arguments about the extensive self were my first encounter with historical phenomenology and the idea that our perception of reality is not fixed and immutable, and that my way of apprehending the world was not the only way. I was not quite comfortable with this. I was excited by the idea because it seemed to make the world a much richer, larger, and more complex place than anyone had ever suggested. I loved the sense of freedom that it seemed to confer. But as a naive realist with an implicit desire for a solid, essentially fundamentalist vision of reality, I was bothered by the suggestion that the modern Western experience of the world is not normative, or perhaps even very common. Surely there are things "out there" about which we have "ideas" and that we describe in "language." We need only look and there they are. I remember asking anxiously "But Mr. Cranz, what about rocks?" My memory is that he smiled his marvelous smile and said that he was a historian and didn't know about rocks.

The answer to this apparent conundrum is only available to those who can learn to close that rift between the soul and the world. Because it is exactly that loss of sympathy, of ontological continuity between our ideas and the things in the world, that gives rise to the "immutable objects" that we have come to think that rocks "really" are.

We have to heal that rift before we can understand that "rocks," in the sense that I meant the word long ago, don't exist at all. By placing the imagination at the center of creation we will come to understand that the desire to find a concrete solidity in which to anchor our sense of the reality of the world and of ourselves starts us on a dangerous path towards the fundamentalist literalism that is the underlying evil of all idolatries, and the root of madness.

But in order to do that we have to rethink the historicist interpretation of the break. I do not think that the "great disjunction," the metaphysical catastrophe that occurred in the twelfth century in Western Europe, was a unique event. The reality must be far more complex. I think that it is, rather, an archetypal event, repeated again and again in various cultures at various times with a range of nuances we cannot easily know, and perhaps more than once in the life of any individual to one degree of severity or another. The break with the world and the loss of sympathy and love occurs over and over in human history. I have no doubt that Cranz and Illich and Corbin have located and described a real event of enormous significance, but it is not unique. Nor was it total, as Corbin at least knew full well. It is on the margins of society that those who carry the flame of the light of illumination have to live. In a moment of youthful enthusiasm he called on the "heretics of the world" to Unite! It is the poets and the mystics, the artists and the dreamers to whom the power of the Imagination has been relegated. They never entirely disappear, they have never been silenced completely. They are the ones who know that the soul is not trapped in history, that on the contrary it is the soul that makes history. And they are the ones we have to turn to if we are to learn the practices of the Imagination. Indeed it is the poets above all who can help us to heal ourselves because it is a disorder of *language* that has been the cause of our isolation.

Cranz writes that the intensive self occupies "a universe of meanings separated by a dichotomy from the world of things." Knowledge derives not from vision and conjunction, but from "*reason* based on the systematic coherence of what is said or thought. [These phases] are held together in the experience of what we call language..."[15] For Hugh of St. Victor it was still possible for the act of reading to be "ontologically remedial" and "bring man to a glow" by breaking through the closed world of "meanings" and opening the human soul to the *anima mundi.* Henry Corbin believed that the history of the West was the story of a great hermeneutic quest to recover the shimmering divine realities hidden behind the opaque and immutable idols which are the literal appearances of things. Behind the literal Words of the Holy Book and obscured by the fixed and literal-minded vision of all the beings in Creation lie numberless openings to the infinite splendor of Creation. He called this quest the search for the *Parole perdu,* the Lost Speech, the Lost Word.

Attention to language is central for any attempt at a therapeutics of our current condition. If many of us exhibit features of the intensive self, and I think we do, then any attempt to recover or reconstitute something like the experience of the extensive self will require work with and on and in language. To awaken a sense of the depth of our immersion in language, and therefore of how deep our research must go, listen to these words of the poet Robert Kelly:

---

15 Cited by Struever in Cranz, *Reorientations of Western Thought,* xii (my italics).

The renewing of our experience through language is a possibility... In the sense that language is the main sea we live in. Although [some people claim that] we live in the body, we live between this body and some other body, and the condition of that between-ness is language. You're not really in your body. You imagine you are in your body but in fact your experiences have to do with your body, my body, her body, this body, that body, objects all around, and the nature of that mediation is language. Language is the ocean in which we live, for any operation in language is an operation in us, too.[16]

Our work will take us deep into that ocean.

In the years since Cranz first proposed his thesis it has come to seem less radical, though his work is little known and his particular notion of the extensive self has not gained many adherents. The idea that different cultures and historical periods construct reality in different ways many now take for granted, and that there should be a historical aspect to cognition and phenomenology is no longing shocking. Not too many perhaps have taken this to its logical conclusion and would agree with Corbin that "ultimately what we call *physis* and the physical is but the reflection of the world of the Soul; there is no pure physics, but always the physics of some definite psychic activity."[17] But if we allow that something like a transition from an extensive to an intensive self, or back again,

---

16 Bradford Morrow, "An Interview with Robert Kelly," *Conjunctions* 13 (Spring 1989) (my italics). Thanks to Pierre Joris for pointing this piece out to me.

17 Corbin, *Spiritual Body and Celestial Earth,* 81.

has occurred, can still occur, or is occurring even now, then what is needed is, first, some means of noticing, and second, methods of influencing it. We have to be able to tell when we begin to lose contact with the freshness of the world, when we no longer feel the strange exhilaration of reality when it is present to us and open, as it is to a child. The first step in freeing yourself from imprisonment is discovering you are in prison. Many people feel some kind of barrier between themselves and the world, as if they live trapped inside a bubble, unable to really *be* here. This feeling of lack and absence and longing is evidence of a deep underlying knowledge of connection, of the primordial human potential for a full and lively immersion in the world, of the intercourse between the human soul and the soul of the world. The cure for the estrangement requires work with language and perception at a very profound level. The alternative is to remain trapped in the restricted and anthropocentric world of merely human meanings, where the "life in sympathy with beings" that Henry Corbin envisioned is not possible.

Henry Corbin and Ivan Illich provide a theological, and in Corbin's case, a mystical perspective on the situation of the human soul and of the experience of language as the essential fabric of Creation. We are immersed in language because everything in existence is God's Word. Not everyone finds this account persuasive. But rather than coming to the ontologically remedial action of language "from above" we can instead, or perhaps *also,* come at it "from below." Seen from this perspective, human language is an entirely natural outcome of the fact that we are biological creatures and it rises up from out of the matter of which we are made. The poet, translator, and mythographer Robert Bringhurst puts this eloquently:

And what is language? Language is what speaks us as well as what we speak. Through our neurons, genes and gestures, shared assumptions and personal quirks, we are spoken by and speak many languages each day, interacting with ourselves, with one another, other species, and the objects—natural and man-made—that populate our world. Even in silence, there is no complete escape from the world of symbols, grammars and signs.[18]

Understood this way language is not a particularly extraordinary attribute of human beings. Making such a claim for human uniqueness immediately and fatally cuts us off from the world, creating a problem that has plagued Western philosophy for centuries.

The poet and ecologist Gary Snyder has pointed out that you simply don't have to do this. The way around the so-called problem of knowledge of the "objective world" is not to try to "solve" it, but just to avoid it entirely. We are not cut off from the world by some peculiar human attribute that isolates us in an impermeable bubble. We are *part* of the world, inextricably in it. The Japanese poet Bashō said: "If you want to learn about the pine, go to the pine." You only learn, Snyder says, by becoming totally absorbed in that which you wish to learn. When Jean-Paul Sartre wrote that there was something absurd about not being able to break through one's skin to get in touch with a tree as we touch it, Snyder says he is at least being honest in confessing

---

18 Robert Bringhurst, *The Solid Form of Language: An Essay On Writing and Meaning* (Kentville, Nova Scotia: Gaspereau Press, 2004), 10-11.

the fundamental sickness of the West.[19] Snyder says that the Japanese poet would reply "There are ways to do it – it is no big deal." He says, "The American Indians and the Japanese are right on the same spot. They both know that it's possible, and that is a major mode of knowledge – to learn about the pine from the pine rather than from a botany book."[20] This is a fine account of the ontological continuity between thing and knowledge characteristic of the extensive self. But it is not so obvious how to attain it if you have already experienced the break and are starting from the position of the intensive self. There has to be a transformation first. That transformation can come about by means of work with language.

Like Bringhurst, David Abram understands human language as an extension of the biological world from which we evolved. He argues persuasively that the break with the world, the great disjunction that gave rise to the intensive self is in fact *caused* by a certain kind of reading, by the cognitive disruptions set in motion by the transition between orality and literacy.[21] His claim is that learning to read a text is such a powerful imaginative experience that it transfers the animation that normally and naturally inheres in our perception of the world around us to the images and feelings that the written text conjures in our mind. Literacy causes a profound rupture in our experience of the world. As the written word gains in its magic power to animate our minds and lives, this animation is drained from the world itself. The

19 Jean-Paul Sartre, *Nausea,* trans. Lloyd Alexander (New York: New Directions, 2013).

20 Gary Snyder, *The Real Work: Interviews & Talks 1964-1979,* ed. W. Scott McLean (New York: New Directions, 1980), 67.

21 David Abram, *The Spell of the Sensuous* (New York: Vintage, 1997).

languages that the world speaks become foreign to us, and we come only to know *our* language. We become trapped in the exclusively human world, and at worst, inside our own heads. In the end we come to live in a world of images, ideas and abstractions rather than flesh and blood and earth and sea and sky. Abram draws on the phenomenology of Heidegger and Merleau-Ponty to show how our abstractions, our concepts, are all ultimately based in physical, sensuous reality. Our embodied lives are the matrix that grounds all of our ideas, all our thinking.

The story is more complex than this outline suggests. It is not really "reading" that is the problem. There was a progressive distancing of the relation between the written sign and the world to which it refers during the long development of writing from pictographs to alphabetic scripts. It is this distancing, the abstraction of the mind from the world, which is the real issue. The development of alphabetic scripts made it possible, but not necessary, to understand human language as a closed system of meanings independent of the nonhuman world. The forms of reflexive, conceptual and abstract reading and thinking that emerged in such a context would form a suitable matrix in which something like the intensive self could appear.

It is not reading and writing *per se* that are the problem, but *certain kinds* of reading and writing and the thinking they enable and display, that exacerbate our isolation. If the world is made of language, conceived either theologically or biologically, then of course humans have always been reading. Bringhurst explains:

> Reading comes first. The reading of tracks and weather signs is a fundamental mammalian occupation, practiced before primates started walking

on their hind legs, much less using hands to write. And writing, in a sense, is always on the verge of being born. All of us who speak by means of gesture, or who gesture as we talk, are gesturing towards writing. But it is a rare event for instincts such as these to crystallize into a system that can capture and preserve the subtleties of speech in graphic form. Such a system can only mature within a culture which is prepared to sustain it. Starting from scratch, with no imported models, people have made the shift from oral to literate culture at least three times but perhaps not many more than that. In Mesopotamia about 5,000 years ago, in northern China about 4,500 years ago, and in Guatemala and southern Mexico about 2,000 years ago, humans created a script and a scribal culture, apparently without imported models of any kind. [22]

Understanding the social and political context is indispensable for grasping the subtle dangers inherent in writing. Its earliest uses were in the service of management and control:

> In each case, the writing began with pictures—which, as they came to stand for words and then for syllables, grew increasingly abstract. In each case, the originating society was already highly organized, with a heavy investment in agriculture, architecture, social institutions and political centralization. And in each case, so far as we can tell, writing was first used in the work of political,

---

22 Bringhurst, *The Solid Form of Language,* 14.

economic or religious administration. Its use for literary purposes came later.[23]

Storytelling, mythmaking, and the recitations of epics all formed the matrix of oral cultures for ages before the invention of writing. But complex societies developed literacy in the service of hierarchical structures of control and domination, not out of any felt need for the enhancement of story, poetry, and song. Bringhurst:

> Writing *in the literary sense* is one of the world's most solitary crafts, but it is only pursued on the margins of highly organized and centralized societies.
>
> Literature – meaning storytelling and poetry – involves the use of language more for purposes of discovery than for purposes of control. It is a part of language itself: present, like language, in every human community. There are no natural languages without stories, just as there are none without sentences. Yet literature is not the cause of writing. Literature *in the written sense* represents the triumph of language over writing: the subversion of writing for purposes that have little or nothing to do with social and economic control.[24]

Written literature is "the triumph of language over writing." Writing was first used for control and domination. This intention results eventually in the dominance of conceptual, abstract thought – what Jung called directed thinking. But in its *literary* infancy writing was in the first

23 Ibid., 15.
24 Ibid., 14-15.

instance a means of making permanent and invariant the living and ever-changing poetry that precedes and infinitely exceeds it. Literary writing is a way of attempting to capture the poetry of the world.

> Sun, moon, mountains and rivers are the writing of being, the literature of what-is. Long before our species was born, the books had been written. The library was here before we were. We live in it. We can add to it, or we can try...
>
> When you think intensely and beautifully, something happens. That something is called poetry. If you think that way and speak at the same time, poetry gets in your mouth. If people hear you it gets in their ears. If you think that way and write at the same time, then poetry gets written. But poetry *exists* in any case. The question is only: are you going to take part, and if so how?[25]

It may be that in some way the controlling, dominating and abstracting tendencies of writing have contaminated all of language for many of us in the modern West. It may have helped to cause the reorientation that gave rise to the intensive self. But we inhabit a literate and complex society and must work with what we have. If writing and reading have been part of the reason we are cut off from the poetry of the world, we know too that reading, and without a doubt writing, can be "ontologically remedial." So we must speak, read and write ourselves back into the world.

The work of the imagination in the processes of reading and writing can be transformational. Again Robert Kelly: "Language is the ocean in which we live, for any

---

25 Robert Bringhurst, *The Tree of Meaning: Language, Mind and Ecology* (Berkeley: Counterpoint, 2008),143.

operation in language is an operation in us, too. And that's what keeps me interested in writing... I want to transform the nature of my experience of the thing I experience."[26] It is this transformation of self and world that we are after here.

There are no doubt many ways to take this arduous and exacting path. I think that any of the arts can surely suffice. But here I want to take another way. If we are concerned with deep transformations in the soul and in language then I think we can do no better than attempt a therapeutics of language, conceptual thought and imagination itself such as is provided by the late, great wizard of depth psychology, James Hillman.

Healing Fictions and the Imagination of Alchemy

James Hillman's wide-ranging and fertile post-Jungian psychology is a powerful source of practically useful psychological knowledge. His contributions to the recovery of the extensive self and the soul of the world, the *anima mundi,* in which such a being lives are without parallel. One of the most important aspects of Hillman's work is his understanding of language. He begins *Healing Fictions* with an extended quote from an interview with Sigmund Freud that is so important that I will present all of it. Freud says:

> Everybody thinks... that I stand by the scientific character of my work and that my principle scope lies in curing mental maladies. This is a terrible error that has prevailed for years and that I have been unable to set right. I am a scientist by necessity, and not by vocation. I am really by nature an

---

26 Morrow, "An Interview with Robert Kelly."

artist... And of this there lies an irrefutable proof: which is that in all countries into which psychoanalysis has penetrated it has been better understood and applied by writers and artists than by doctors. My books, in fact, more resemble works of imagination than treatise on pathology... I have been able to win my destiny in an indirect way, and have attained my dream: to remain a man of letters, though still in appearance a doctor. In all great men of science there is a leaven of fantasy, but no one proposes like to me to translate the inspirations offered by the currents of modern literature into scientific theories. In psychoanalysis you may find fused together thought changed into scientific jargon, the three greatest literary schools of the nineteenth century: Heine, Zola, and Mallarmé are united in me under the patronage of my old master, Goethe.[27]

So, Hillman tells us, right at the very foundation, in the work of Freud,

Psychoanalysis is a work of imaginative tellings in the realm of *poiesis,* which means simply "making," and which I take to mean making by imagination in words. Our work... belongs to the *rhetoric* of poiesis, by which I mean the persuasive power of imagining in words, an artfulness in speaking and hearing, writing and reading.[28]

---

27 Giovanni Papini, "A Visit to Freud," *Review of Existential Psychology and Psychiatry* 9, no. 2 (1969): 130-34; quoted in James Hillman, *Healing Fiction* (Putnam, Conn: Spring Publications, 2009), 3.

28 Hillman, *Healing Fiction,* 3-4.

This work with language is a principle *cultural* task that has as one aim the unification of psyche and logos. Words that lie dormant within and are not breathed into life and given some play on stage, cannot heal the wounds that cripple and isolate the soul. Words, to be animate, filled with anima, must have breath and body and a public airing. There is no private language. Hillman writes,

> Freud's "talking cure" is also the cure of our talk, an attempt at that most difficult of cultural tasks, the rectification of language: the right word... A mark of imaginal man is the speech of his soul, and the range of this speech... can be supplanted neither by the technology of communication media, by contemplative spiritual silence, nor by physical gestures and signs. The more we hold back from the risk of speaking because of the semantic anxiety that keeps the soul in secret incommunicado, private and personal, the greater grows the credibility gap between what we are and what we say, splitting psyche and logos.[29]

Psychotherapy then attends to the rhetoric of the soul, to the stories we tell and that we tell ourselves, to the constant undercurrent, the murmur of speech that enacts, explains and interprets our lives and ours worlds, and of which we are for the most part unaware. Any therapy that helps uncover these acts and interpretations is therefore a *hermeneutic* discipline.

In a pivotal move Hillman calls on Alfred Adler's hermeneutic understanding of mental illness. We ask: What distinguishes between the normal, the neurotic and the

29 James Hillman, *Re-Visioning Psychology* (New York: Harper and Row, 1975), 217.

psychotic? Both Freud and Jung give systematic, scientific explanations. But, says Hillman,

> Adler gives a *hermeneutic* explanation... madness is a matter of interpretation, a delusional poiesis – truly a *mental* disease, *psychic* disorder, an account of which cannot be put into objective terms.
>
> Adler says: "I readily follow the ingenious views of Vaihinger,[30] who maintains that historically ideas tend to grow from *fictions*...to *hypotheses*...and later to *dogmas*. This change of intensity differentiates in a general way the thinking of the normal individual (fiction as expedient), of the neurotic (attempt to realize the fiction) and of the psychotic (...reification of the fiction...)."[31]

In other words, "What makes madness," Hillman says, "is literalism." And then the therapy, the cure for madness, is another hermeneutic strategy:

> If the progression from sanity towards mental illness is distinguished by degrees of literalism, then the therapeutic road from psychosis back to sanity is one of going back through the same hermeneutic passage – deliteralizing.[32]

This is the move that frees us from dogma and fundamentalism – from the certainty that kills the soul and the spirit. This is the hermeneutic move leading thought and things back to the virtualities of the imagination, back to the archetypal matrix that gives them life.

---

30 Hans Vaihinger (1852-1933); see his *Philosophy of As If* (1911).
31 Hillman, *Healing Fiction,* 111.
32 Ibid.

But there is yet another step, another release that is necessary. And this step into freedom is hard to make. We have to give up the paired literalisms of the individual ego and the ego psychology that attempts to cure it. We have to give up our attachment to psychology itself, to the literalism of psychotherapeutics. Here is the really radical heart of Hillman's psychology. He reminds us of one of Henry Corbin's central themes: it is not my individuation that is the issue, but the individuation of the angel. Hillman's life work can perhaps be read as an extended attack on ego psychology based on the revelation that psychology, the logos of soul, is not only a study of the human, but opens essentially onto the more-than-human surround in which we are embedded: is it the world soul, the *anima mundi,* that is the subject of this mode of knowing. It is the world we are engaged in saving – not ourselves, not *my* individual soul. That *cannot* be enough – the hope for a salvation of the isolated individual, or even of all merely human beings, is a delusion and itself in need of revisioning. We and the communal language through which we live and breathe and imagine are part of a fabric of which we are ever only dimly aware. That is why we must speak of the ecology of the psyche and of the more-than-human context for all that we are.

Language is utterly ubiquitous, and as natural as earth, air, fire, and water. Its domain includes the depths of the soul to be sure, but it also permeates the surfaces of everything we touch. Speech and sign are everywhere. This is why *depth* is not the only or even the best metaphor for meaning. The very notion of depth psychology suggests that we must always go deep to find the meaning of things. This would be the source of Hillman's discomfort with the Germanic, serious, sober side of psychology and his glee in moving to the Mediterranean with Vico, Ficino and the Renaissance Neoplatonists. The poet Robert Duncan says in a rather tongue-in-cheek way that what we need isn't really depth psychology but shallow psychology. In a bit of a rant against a contemptuous critic of Denise Levertov, who sneered at the mythic, the mysterious, and the aura of the sacred in her work, Duncan writes,

> Everywhere there is the ready suspicion and accusation that the poet has not really earned or deserved to have wonder manifest in the poem, as if wonder came from some power of the writer's and was not a grace recognized by the writer in the reality of things. The world is then filled with "prosaic" things... that do not deserve our poetic attentions, or that need to be seen as deep images of the psyche before they become poetic. As things in themselves they won't work.[33]

The point as I take it – and I find this a marvelous and great gift – is that we don't *always* need to dig deep, to furrow our brows and plunge into the depths to find the poetic shimmer in the world. The surfaces of the normal things of life are wondrous, and meaningful enough. The things in themselves *do* work. But I think it remains true that *seeing* this may require a long and difficult work of redemption. It is the seeing of the extensive self, and you might have to go pretty deep before you can see the light on the surfaces of things.

The redemption of the prosaic is one goal of the hermeneutics of the world that we are engaged in as we attempt to reconstitute something like an extensive self. Jung has shown us that *alchemy* is at root a process for

---

33 "The Truth and Life of Myth," in *Fictive Certainties: Essays by Robert Duncan* (New York: New Directions, 1985), 25.

the redemption of the mundane, prosaic, material world. It happens that we are part of that world—a world that is as much soul and spirit as it is matter. And it is I think in their alchemical writings that we find both Jung and Hillman at the height of their magnificent, profound powers of creative imagination. I think it is in Hillman's writings on alchemy that he finds his most powerful and effective voice. Duncan thought that in this work he was coming very close indeed to poetry.[34]

The alchemical interpretation of psychic processes was pioneered by Jung, who recognized his own inner turmoil in the chaotic and wildly imaginative texts of the alchemists. Alchemical metaphors get right to the heart of the *prima materia* of emotional life in all its pain, confusion, density, and complexity. It provides a language and a method for an intense struggle with perception and emotion that can lead to the understanding of the complexes that structure and control the greater part of our intellectual and emotional life. The alchemical process for all its chaos and nearly infinite variety consists of movements of the psyche back and forth across the boundaries of consciousness and over the contours of the emotions. In this way the contours and the contents of the soul become ever more conscious, for boundaries alone reveal the shape of the psyche, and alchemical language provides a description of the expeditions across the margins and into the interiors of the soul. The alchemical process also requires intense work with perception itself since perception is hardly the passive reception of sensory data that the empiricists believed but is soaked with emotion and guided by the images that flood the psyche. Only *changes* in perception reveal the nature

---

34 Robert Duncan, "Opening the Dreamway," *Spring: A Journal of Archetype and Culture* 59 (1996), 35.

of experience, and close attention to the subtle varieties of perception help open the doors to the wider world.

I want to provide a bit of commentary on Hillman's crucial essay on alchemical language. He tells us that there are three main ways that alchemy is relevant for analytical psychology. It provides a grounding for Jung's theory; it provides a phenomenology for practice; and alchemical language itself is therapeutic:

> Besides the general theory of alchemical transformation and besides the particular parallels of alchemical imagery with the individuation process, it is *alchemical language* that may be most valuable for Jungian therapy. Alchemical language itself is a mode of therapy; it is itself therapeutic.[35]

He says that to talk therapy we must talk about neurosis. Neurosis we take to be a one-sided development of personality. And the neurosis

> resides in the patterns of our conscious personality organization, in the habitual ways we go about our days... [It] is located right in one's conscious framework... I am neurotic because of what goes on here and now, as I stand and look and talk, rather than what went on once, or goes in society, or in my dreams, fantasies, emotions, memories, symptoms. My neurosis resides in my mental set

---

35 James Hillman, "The Therapeutic Value of Alchemical Language: A Heated Introduction," in *Alchemical Psychology,* Uniform Edition of the Writings of James Hillman, vol. 5 (Putnam, Conn.: Spring Publications, 2014), 10.

and the way it constructs the world and behaves in it.[36]

Since we live in language as fish live in water, Hillman can say "If I am neurotic I am neurotic in language." Since language is a social phenomenon, the one-sidedness of neurotic language will generally reflect that of the culture. The collective language of modern Western culture is founded on "directed thinking," as Jung showed and Hillman has long emphasized. Conceptual language is the rhetorical style of this directed thinking – as it is the rhetorical style of the *ego*, that master of direction and control. Hillman says conceptual language "is the chronic locus of our collective neurosis as it appears in language."[37]

The concept is the workhorse of rationalism. Rationalism accounts for the world in concept words rather than images or thing words or craft words. It is based on establishing identities – what something *is* rather than what it is *like.* And to say what something *is* we have to treat it schematically, abstractly, since the *real thing itself* is far too complex, individual and immediate to *be* anything but itself. So we take this *being* away from it, and rather than describing it metaphorically, we categorize it with a concept and say what it *is.* So, Hillman says, we may claim that our hypotheses and conceptual statements are only heuristic, but in practice was substantiate everything because we are trapped in the literalism of our language. Of the rationalism of psychology he writes,

> We speak in concepts: the ego and the unconscious; libido, energy and drive; opposites, regression, feeling-function, compensation, transference

---

36 Ibid.
37 Ibid., 11.

...When working with these terms we curiously forget they are concepts only, barely useful for grasping psychic events which they inadequately describe.[38]

That is, many of us, if not most of us, tend to be literalists: there is no "as if" between our language and what it is meant to be conceiving. Our concepts become real things. Hillman puts it this way:

Substantives become substances. So much so that we consider these concepts able to account for personality and its neuroses, whereas I am arguing that these very same substantialized concept terms – ego, unconscious, transference – *are* the neurosis.[39]

This is where alchemy comes in. Its therapeutic function is to help us deliteralize the way we think about the psyche, the activities of soul and the world beyond the limits of the human.

It has taken me a long time to accept this move entirely seriously. You really have to dig pretty deep, if you are a conceptual rationalist, to get below, or beyond, all those defensive concepts – the constructs of the mind that structure and filter experience and make it safe for human consumption. It is not that concepts must be banished. Only they must not be taken literally – the "things" they posit are not substances, they are not real beings that we have discovered. They may be the traces, the markings, the skins of such beings – but even then they are to be grasped very lightly. Henry Corbin puts it nicely when he says that

38 Ibid., 12.
39 Ibid.

the logical concept is only the dead body of an Angel. Concepts are at best the empty husk left behind when the living being they attempt to represent has fled. Conceptual rationalism by itself leads at best to an impoverished and incomplete experience of life.

Now what is it that alchemical language offers that is better than concepts and abstractions? Well, to begin with, Hillman says "thing-words, image-words, craft-words. The five supposed sources of alchemy is each a technology. Each is a handwork physically grappling with sensate materials."[40] These sources are: metallurgy, the dyeing of fibers, embalming the dead, perfumery and cosmetics, and pharmacy. To these he importantly adds the preparation and cooking of foods. All of the operations are based in physical experience and all carried and still carry meanings about nature:

> The basic stuffs of personality—salt, sulfur, mercury and lead—are concrete materials...The words for alchemical vessels—the shapes of soul in which our personality is being worked—contrast with the concepts we use...alchemy presents an array of different qualities of vessel... One uses copper or glass or clay to hold one's stuff and cook it.
>
> Finally, the worlds for the operations...are again concrete...We learn about condensing and congealing...coagulating and fixing, about dissolving and putrefying, about mortifying and blackening.[41]

---

40 Ibid., 13.
41 Ibid., 13-14.

In contrast, the conceptual language of psychology is not only abstract, but it is imprecise. And "because of this imprecision...we have come to believe the soul itself is an ungraspable flux, whereas actually the psyche presents itself always in very specific behaviors, experiences and sensuous images."[42]

And yet the specificity and concreteness of alchemical imagery and language must not be confused with literalism and univocity of meaning:

> Alchemy leaves unilateral literalism completely. No term means only one thing. Every alchemical phenomenon is both material and psychological at the same time, else alchemy could not claim to be salvific of both the human soul and material nature. It is all metaphor...All analogy. All a *poiesis* of the hand.[43]

Hillman points out that ever since Jung introduced alchemy into psychology, people have tended to translate the alchemical imagination into direct, conceptual thought. So the White Queen and the Red King become masculine and feminine principles and the Stone and a variety of other images become symbols of the Self and so on. But, we could do this differently. If we understand our concepts only as potentially heuristic metaphors and not signs for substantive realities, then we might not need to leave the alchemical language at all. "We could speak to the dreams as the dreams themselves speak." Or we could respond to behaviors and fantasies as if they were dreams, as if they were alchemical operations, apparatuses and substances. We

---

42 Ibid., 14.
43 Ibid., 14-15.

must speak "dreamingly, imagistically, and – materially."[44] We might, that is to say, speak *poetically*.

And here is Hillman's decisive insight. It seems to me of unsurpassed importance. We must speak *materially* he says. That is the power of alchemy – it is a theory and a practice of the redemption of matter. It embraces a world view in which language has body, images have body, soul has body – and these bodies, subtle though they may be, are required if the world we think of as material is to have any body at all. The subtle bodies of language, soul, and image are required to counteract the abstractions of conceptual thought and of the spirit. Concepts have to be *both* deliteralized *and* materialized. *It is the literal that is abstract.* The real world is far too rich, complex, and manifold to ever be encompassed by any literalism. Literalism is the root of disembodiment and the meaninglessness of nihilism. There is in fact no literal language – there is only language that we attempt to understand literally.

Now I would want to argue that alchemical language is a subset of poetic language, but it is a particularly clear and compelling example of the power of poetic imagination. I quote Hillman at length on alchemy:

> Its beauty lies just in its materialized language, which we can never take literally. I know I am not composed of sulfur and salt, buried in horse dung, putrefying or congealing, turning white or green or yellow, encircled by a tail-biting serpent, rising on wings. And yet I am! I cannot take any of this literally, even if it is all accurate, descriptively true. Even while the words are concrete, material, physical, it is a patent mistake to take them literally.

---

44 Ibid., 15.

Alchemy gives us a language of substance which cannot be taken substantively, concrete expressions which are not literal.

This is its therapeutic effect: it forces metaphor upon us. We are carried by the language into an as-if, into both the materialization of the psyche and the psychization of matter as we utter our words.[45]

Alchemical language forces metaphor upon us. It requires the deliteralization of thought and language. It places the imagination at the center of reality.

Now we have to take care not to merely use alchemical language as if it were a substitute for the conceptual terms of psychology. Hillman proposes not a literal return to alchemy but rather to an alchemical mode of speech and imagination. That is to say: to take seriously the rhetoric and style, the images and sentences of the dream and the daydream and the mood; to take seriously the feelings of the soul in its everydayness as well as in its extremities. To pay attention to everything that is going on – that is the goal. It is in practice impossible – the vastness of the present moment prevents it. We ignore so very much. And we tend to ignore the same things all the time until they force themselves upon us. All the subtle, fleeting moods, images, sensations. To let them in we have to open our attention and this requires breaking out of the boxes that literal language constructs for us.[46] And so, alchemy –

---

45 Ibid., 16.

46 Heidegger was onto this is his own way–his analyses of moods in *Being and Time* (1927) are not *that* far removed from the concern with soul that Jung was outlining in the *Red Book* at roughly the same time.

because it *cannot* be taken literally, but forces metaphor and poetry on us.

We are in fact living in a state of imagination all the time. For "literalizing" itself is a mode of imagining – it is the mode characteristic of Spirit, Hillman argues, and so we find it most commonly in science, theology and metaphysics. What makes imagination *active* is being able to move among styles of imagining in the great flux of metaphors, never stuck too long in any one mode. So we need to acknowledge the fact of our constant and unavoidable imagining by making it active, fluid and alive. This is the point – alchemical imagining as Hillman describes it is Jung's "active imagination." A return to the imagination of alchemy as a therapeutic technique means an expanded vision of what active imagination can be: it returns all of life to the imagination. Then, when we are most literal, most stuck, most in pain, we can know that all of it, all the confusion and anguish is being held within that larger, more fluid and meaningful whole.

Critical is the knowledge, foundational for alchemy, that all of these imaginings are *material* and embodied. Again: the literal is not the concrete. These are habitually confounded. The reality is quite the opposite. *It is abstraction which is literal; the concrete is always imaginal.* Only an abstraction can be so simple as to be understood literally. Concrete, immediate reality always exceeds the bounds of our possible knowledge – it is *saturated* with reality.[47] To understand this we need to expand our sense of what "body" signifies precisely by means of the metaphoric view

---

47 I borrow Jean-Luc Marion's evocative term of "saturated phenomena" (see his *In Excess: Studies of Saturated Phenomena*, trans. Robyn Horner and Vincent Berraud [New York: Fordham University Press, 2004]).

of life. Bodies come in uncountable types and styles—a range of rhetorics must apply. Some are heavy, dark and solid, others feather-like, luminous and subtle; others exhibit all the possible ranges in between. This is what we should have in mind when we speak, in that most Christian of metaphors, of the Word made Flesh.

In a magnificent essay on the color blue in alchemical psychology, Hillman arrives finally, after long passages through desire and depression and despair, at this description of the first goal of the alchemical opus, the union of logos and psyche:

> We are arriving at the essence of the *unio mentalis*: the transformation of imagination, and a radical shift in the very idea of imagination. After the despair of blue and the desire of blue, the inventive virtuosity of this force has so saturated our hearts and sight with a heaven- or hell-sent sense of life, imagination having become so pervasive a power, it can no longer be confined to a mental function or conceived as one psychological capacity among others. In fact, imagination can no longer belong to human psychology, but must like grace be accorded archetypal attribution, something descended into our lives from an imaginal realm.[48]

When this happens, it liberates the soul to range freely and widely in all the spaces of the world, in all the realms of language, from the genetic code and the love language

---

48 Hillman, "Alchemical Blue and the *Unio Mentalis*," in *Alchemical Psychology*, 116.

of the sandhill cranes to the emerald cities and angelic hierarchies of the *mundus imaginalis*. All of it has reality, of many different kinds, but not *literal* reality, not the opaque, immutably fixed reality of an idol. But this is not quite right, for even now there will be times of darkness and fixation, idolatry and truculent certainty. But these will be impermanent, and bedded in the greater enveloping reality of the flow of the Imagination. This world does not emerge from a meaningless material substrate according to the laws of Newton or Darwin or Freud where imagination and love, poetry and music are but epiphenomena of natural selection or the repressions of libido. Nor is it hung suspended from God above as from a single fixed point over an abyss of nothingness from which the creatures flee in terror towards the Light. It is not a world to escape but to inhabit. The choice is not between horizontal and vertical, immanence and transcendence, darkness and light. Nothing so simple is offered us. No such straightforward mapping of reality will suffice. Neither horizontal nor vertical makes any sense without the other. Together they merely hint at the living realities of a complex and heterogeneous space. So, too, with immanence and transcendence: each constellates and requires the other, and both are present everywhere and always across all the scales of time and space. And so too with darkness and light. The living world is mostly chiaroscuro. But here there is another caution. As Corbin tells us, there are two kinds of darkness. The dark light of the divine mystery penetrates everything in creation. The darkness of evil is something else entirely. The two not always easily distinguished. The simple pairs of opposites are at most coordinates that may help us orient ourselves. They have the range and richness of archetypes, but we should heed Hillman's warning and take care not to empty them and render them destructive by using them as *concepts,* because then they will inflate into vague and misleading *abstractions.* If we slothfully slacken our attention to the challenges of the wildness and richness of the world it is, then these lively opposing forces are only apprehended as caricatures and so degenerate into idols. The world we inhabit is opulent and complex, surprising, confusing and creative through and through. If these pairs of opposites are to have any use at all we need to imagine ourselves and all the beings of the world as suspended in dynamic tension between them, living in mystery and ambiguity. But the result is not *dis*-orientation as some may fear. What truly orients us is not an abstract concept, or even an archetype. For they are impersonal. What orients us is *longing.* Corbin describes it as an energy of nostalgia that fills the universe, and that is the soul's secret source of energy for the operation of any spiritual hermeneutics, and alchemy is hermeneutics *par excellence.* Alchemy is the work of the redemption of matter, and so, of our bodies, saving them from the idolatry of literalism and recognizing them in their true home in the imaginal world of mystery and ceaseless creation. The goal of this transformative operation in language is the continuous Incarnation of the Word.

3

The Middle Voice

Mundus Imaginalis

In a 1980 interview, James Hillman spoke about the fanaticism that often characterizes single-vision consciousness and the totalitarian forms of religion that it produces. Every religion has extremists, but it is perhaps easier to find them shocking in an exotic and foreign faith. Hillman recalled a conversation with Henry Corbin:

> Corbin said to me one time, "What is wrong with the Islamic world is that it has destroyed its images, and without these images that are so rich in its tradition, they are going crazy because they have no containers for their extraordinary imaginative power." His work with mystical philosophical texts, the texts that re-establish the imaginal world, can be seen as political action of the first order: it was meeting terrorism, fanaticism, nihilism right at its roots in the psyche.[1]

Corbin died in 1978, the year of Khomeini's Islamic Revolution in Iran. I assume that Iranian unrest provides the context for Corbin's remarks. It would be willful blindness to ignore the fact that the revolution was brought on in large part by American and British complicity in deposing Mossadegh and installing the Shah. Corbin's comment could

---

1 James Hillman, *Inter Views: Conversations with Laura Pozzo* (Dallas: Spring Publications, 1983), 142-43.

be read as a sign of his naiveté regarding political reality. But even if Corbin was blind to the political dimension of religion, that does not negate the power of his imaginative vision to counteract the forces of extremism. The challenges of fundamentalist religion are now more evident than ever as the tensions continue to mount in the relations among Jews, Christians, and Muslims in the Middle East and throughout the world.

But the fundamentalist phenomenon as I want to think about it is broader than that and encompasses any of the "isms" that we may embrace: capitalism, communism, racism, sexism, and on and on. I am thinking of fundamentalism as a fixation and inflexibility that may manifest variously in the mind, the heart and the body. I want to think of it as a kind of excessive closure that originates in the normal and necessary boundaries that structure each and every one of us. It becomes pathological to the degree that it closes off the world and cramps and cripples our responsiveness, our abilities to think and feel and move in response to a manifold and changing surround. It constricts and limits the range of options, it constrains our freedom and the creative potential that we have to interpret and experience the world. It is a pathology of our normal boundary conditions. The body is both open to the world and closed off from it. Normally, we breathe in rhythms of inspiration and expiration. In a variety of ways we take in portions of the world, let it pass through us and out again, letting it transform us by its transit. Biologically it is obvious that any prolonged cessation of this passage of the world into, through, and out of us again results in death. The same is true of the heart and the mind. Perhaps we can think of fundamentalism as a stifling, an asphyxiation, and constipation of the soul.

This common pathology has its roots in the powerful emotions that flow through most of us daily and that may peak in moments of anger and rigidity, defensiveness and fear, but if all goes well, then ebb naturally and disappear, leaving little overt damage in their wake. We cannot understand any form of extremism if we do not feel it as similar in kind to aspects of our own quite "normal" personality. Fanaticism and extremism are our own impulsive and compulsive angers and passions raised to a higher pitch and given an architecture rendering them more coherent and more systematic. Then they seem not merely the urges of private inner demons, but wear a public face that can be displayed and marketed to an audience. Regarding extremism and fanaticism as exotic and shocking makes of them foreign and incomprehensible behaviors that can only be seen from the outside, and as we like to say, "objectively." But such a public, impersonal viewpoint depersonalizes and dehumanizes the very inhumanity we hope to confront. Then we either look down upon it from a viewpoint of arrogant superiority and fail to engage it at all; or we rage against it as an external alien Other and risk becoming the monsters that we project. The inhuman can only be countered by knowing it as the human – by seeing it "subjectively" in its interiority, and personalizing it. Only then can it be worked at psychologically, from the inside.

Hillman says that Henry Corbin's work to re-establish the reality of the imaginal world "can be seen as political action of the first order: it [is] meeting terrorism, fanaticism, nihilism right at [their] roots in the psyche." I want to try to get at those roots, to work into that tangle. To begin: what is the imaginal world? Or, more to the point, what is it like to live in it? But that's not quite the right question either. There is no imaginal world somewhere out there that we can visit. Entry into the imaginal signals not a change of place, but a change in your mode of being. Just as finding one's "soul" is not the discovery of a thing but a deepening of experience, so entering the Imaginal involves a fundamental transformation in the condition of the world. It involves a kind of opening. And, mystics tell us, the openings go on forever. Now I am certainly no mystic, and what little I know of the imaginal involves really rather small openings. These may begin subtly and without fanfare, though they are in my experience often hard won. In my own case the initial openings were in fact rather dramatic and unexpected, but this was apparently necessary to get my attention, which was, as is the case for most people, pretty much devoted to other things. From then on however, it seems you have to work rather hard for it.

The openings require a loosening of your attention and relaxing of your intentions – you have to stop grasping at the world. You have to come to feel that nothing is *literal* – nothing is only what it seems on the surface. Everything has depth, breadth, and extended reference. The world is a vast and intricate web of correspondences. In particular we have to know that the inner and the outer are not disjunct. To use the terminology of metaphysics, what we call the "subjective" is "ontologically continuous" with the "objective" world. Poets and artists assume this to be true. Some people seem not to be able to let the world melt in quite this way. Scientists claim to strive after the literal, objective reality of the world, but much of the time they fail miserably and the results of their looking are connections and wonders and beauties no one had known before. Certain kinds of intellectual activities do try to hold the outer world still and keep it simple, and they have their uses. Single vision can be helpful in the sciences and engineering sometimes. But any really creative life of the mind and heart is always based on what Blake called "double vision."[2] For Henry Corbin this meant being able to see the divine light shining through all things. The world takes on a kind of transparency. I would follow James Hillman and argue that it is better to say "multiple vision," since speaking only of double vision suggests a too simple contrast between immanence and transcendence that is not always very helpful. We fall into a network of correspondences and the distinction between the transcendent and the immanent seems often a hindrance to the imagination.

Mostly what prevents our opening to the richness and complexity of the world is not intellectual hesitation or inadequate critical distinctions but a dysfunction and crippling of the emotions. It is, as Jung would have it, usually the feeling function that is out of order. We wall off portions of our inner life because they hurt. It happens unconsciously for the most part, and for a while it works. But because everything is connected in unknown and unpredictable ways the frozen parts of our life begin to spread. Cramped, crippled, dead, and cold—whole terrains of our experience begin to solidify. This is one way that literalism begins to dominate the imagination. And static imagination is not imagination at all—it is dogma and ideology. It gives rise to idolatry. The world becomes opaque as our emotional responses narrow in range and become automatic reflexes. In an opaque world the boundaries of everything are clear and distinct. We know where we stand. We know the facts. My mother is a witch. My boss is an ogre. My neighbor is a fool. My wife is a nag. My mistress is Aphrodite. My god is great. You see how

2 "For double the vision my eyes do see, / And a double vision is always with me." (William Blake in a letter to Thomas Butts, 22 November 1802)

attractive this is. It is simple, clear, and reliable. You never have to move outside your comfort zone.

This story oversimplifies, but I think there is truth enough to make it useful. Whatever the social and political context, idolatry, fundamentalism and literalism have in common a monotheism of consciousness that is grounded in a lack of imagination that is in turn based very often in pain and fear. It seems that when the imagination withdraws from some areas of experience it may hypertrophy in others. Thus we find poets and artists with disastrous personal lives, or people who try to find solace in what we call escapism in literature or in the movies. But the effects will appear somewhere. Recall Corbin's claim that the people of the Islamic world had lost contact with their extraordinary imagination, and those uncontrolled forces were driving them crazy.

There is a tight complementarity between the emotions and the imagination. The imagination is a powerful solvent – it keeps things fluid and prevents the world from freezing up. It breaks down walls. It refuses the literal and sees all things as metaphoric and symbolic. Imagination perceives correspondences. To do this it must flow. It is the essential element for any work with the crippled and uncontrolled emotions that dominate the literalist psyche. The emotions all have their own dynamic and style of imagination, but when they are dominant, monolithic, autonomous, and automatic it is as if the whole person has been caught in some vast eddy of energy, cut off from the broader stream and unable to escape. Jung had a name for these reflexive, habitual and semi-conscious emotions that so often dominate our lives. They are the *feeling-toned complexes*. The great challenge of psychic development is to become conscious of the complexes that dominate your life. It is the great work – the *magnum opus*. And I think the one of the best ways to think about the process involved is by means of the metaphors of alchemy.

The psychic and spiritual battles that alchemy describes are difficult and painful almost beyond description. The *prima materia* of the opus consists in a *massa confusa* of wild emotions – a powerful chaos of pain, shame, rage, fear, anger, hatred, and anguish. All of it must be contained in the *vas bene clausum* – a well-sealed vessel, and a veritable furnace. For the impossible rule of this work is "don't repress; don't act out" – the only allowable action is to stay sealed in the furnace and Imagine. In the heat at the heart of the great work the cooking occurs by means of a series of operations repeated over and over again in a seemingly endless process of psychosomatic stresses and transformations. The goal is to get some distance between the soul in the oven and the dominating and impersonal emotions that engulf her. The struggle is to discover that the all-consuming passions, whatever they are, are not inevitable responses to features of some stable, objective world but states of the psyche – and so, the world they arise in response to is not literal and objective, not permanent, not the Truth. This distancing is the difficult process of becoming conscious of a complex. It is the chief key to freedom from the passions. Only through this distancing, the dis-identification with the complex, can clarity be had in any emotional situation. And the one certain rule here, so very hard to keep front and center, is that any time there is strong affect, any time the passions rage, there is a complex at the center of the storm.

The passions of the fundamentalist psyche for order, truth, certainty, and conformity, when they are expressed with the unyielding fanaticism of the extremist, are inexplicable without the psychological insight that complex psychology and the therapeutic tools of the alchemical understanding of psyche can provide. This is in no way a denial of the social and political causes of religious extremism. But lacking work at the level of the psyche, no political solutions to any of the current conflicts can be expected to be adequate. This gives a new meaning to the saying of the first imam of the Shi'ites that Corbin so often quoted: Alchemy is the Sister of Prophecy. Prophetic religion without alchemy is blind, unconscious, and incomplete, destined to descend into fanaticism and idolatry. But in the vision of Henry Corbin it is the love and beauty at the heart of the Creative Imagination that unites the grand sweep of the Prophetic Tradition from Moses through Jesus to Mohammed and beyond.

We can now think a bit about how we might conceive of the essential unity of the religions of the Abrahamic tradition – the Religions of the Book.

The Angel of the Middle Voice

Anyone who first learns of Islam from a genuine Sufi or from one of the many Sufi-inspired writers on the subject cannot help being struck by the inherent pluralism that characterizes the faith. The Qur'an, which Muslims consider the unmediated Word of God, puts it this way:

> Surely the believers and the Jews, the [Christians] and the Sabians, whoever believes in God and the Last Day, and whosoever does right, shall have his reward with his Lord, and will have neither fear nor regret.[3]

---

3 *Al-Qur'an,* trans. Ahmed Ali (Princeton, N.J.: Princeton University Press, 1984), 2:62. The Qur'anic term for Christians is "Nazareans."

According to Ibn 'Arabī, the great twelfth-century mystic from Islamic Spain, the infinite God so transcends the created cosmos and any of our thoughts about Him that his Infinity can only be expressed through a vast multiplicity of revelations. There is no Absolute in this world. The Absolute can only be expressed through relativity. The obviousness of this often seems stunning to me, but it is certainly not so to many people. The idea that God must speak with many voices is of central importance for any attempt to save the monotheistic tradition from the domination of Single Vision and a pathological monotheism of consciousness. The Gospel of John in the New Testament opens with this: "In the beginning was the Word. And the Word was with God, and the Word was God."[4] Christ, understood as the second person of the Trinity in later theology, is that Word. But in some varieties of the mystical tradition the emphasis is on the withdrawal of Christ – we have lost the Word, and each of us must work to reclaim it. The American poet Robert Duncan, whose work is in profound sympathy with Henry Corbin's vision of the imagination, begins his book on his friend and mentor H.D. with a quote from A.E. Waite's 1924 book on the Rosicrucians. Here the connection between the Word and the multitude of voices of the cosmos is made evident. The recovery of the Voice is a glorious dawn:

> As regards the Lost Word, it is explained that the sun at autumn has lost its power and Nature is rendered mute, but the star of day at the spring tide resumes its vital force, and this is the recovery of the Word, when Nature with all her voices, speaks and sings, even as the Sons of God shouted for joy in the perfect morning of the cosmos.[5]

---

4 John 1:1.
5 A.E. Waite, *The Brotherhood of the Rosy Cross, Being Records*

Henry Corbin may well have struck upon the idea of the Lost Word from his reading of Waite. In any case it is in perfect harmony with his theological scheme. The symbol of the dawn occurs throughout Corbin's work, based as it is on a Neoplatonic philosophy of Illumination. And Corbin is happy to find the signs and voices of God's language in all the beings of Creation in accordance with Qur'anic teachings. But for Corbin it is also the *Parole perdue,* the Lost Word or Lost Speech that provides the unifying metaphor that links all the religions of Abraham together:

> The drama common to all the "religions of the Book"…can be designated as the drama of the "Lost Speech." And this because the whole meaning of their life revolves around the phenomenon of the revealed holy Book, around the true meaning of this Book. If the true meaning of the Book is the interior meaning, hidden under the literal appearance, then from the instant that men fail to recognize or refuse this interior meaning, from that instant they mutilate the unity of the Word…and begin the drama of the "Lost Speech."[6]

This hidden meaning of the Word of God is available in principle to everyone. But not in the same way that the literal meaning is. The literal meaning is the public meaning, shared by definition by every believer. The inner meaning

---

of the House of the Holy Spirit in Its Inward and Outward History (London: Rider, 1924), 430; quoted in Robert Edward Duncan and Michael Boughn, *The H.D. Book: The Collected Writings of Robert Duncan* (Berkeley: University of California Press, 2011), 35.

6 "L'initiation ismaélienne ou l'ésotérisme et le verbe," in Henry Corbin, *L'Homme et son ange: initiation et chevalerie spirituelle* (Paris: Fayard, 1983), 81.

is as real, as true, as the "objective" meaning, but it is by definition *individual* and available to each person *alone*. It cannot be made objective and public. It requires a personal revelation – it requires the act of an angel. Each of us stands alone before the face of the Divine. But God in His Majesty never reveals Himself as such – the Absolute remains absolute. Mediation is required, and the mediators are the Angels. There is an Angel of Revelation for each of us. Or, the Angel of Revelation pluralizes itself and shatters gloriously, as it must, into an infinity of Faces – each absolute for the person to whom it is revealed. Thus Christ, as the Word Who appears to everyone, is not the literal historical figure of mainstream dogmatic theology. He is, rather, an angel of infinite Faces. Corbin denies the reality of the Incarnation. His Christology is Islamic and his radically heretical Christianity is a post-Islamic, or he would argue, a pre-Conciliar Christianity, rejecting the dogma of the Council of Nicea, and looking back to the angel Christology of some early Christians.

In the scheme of this theological anthropology each human person is composed of two parts: the earthly and the heavenly. Each of us has a heavenly Twin, a Celestial figure who is the guarantor of our eternal individuality and our connection with the divine. If this connection is broken we are lost. We can make it stronger by searching for our divine counterpart, or it can be destroyed by ignorance or willful neglect or rejection. We think we are independent individuals. We worship the active, dominant ego. But Corbin says "the active subject is in reality not you, your autonomy is a fiction. In reality, you are the subject of a verb in the passive (you are the *ego* of a *cogitor*)."[7] We are, to the degree

---

7 Henry Corbin, *Creative Imagination in the Sufism of Ibn 'Arabī,*

that the connection remains strong, made whole and complete by the action of the Angel in us and through us. Only when this link is destroyed do we become truly independent, and then we are indeed lost "in vagabondage and perdition" as mortal, finite, and fragmented beings.

This means that the central concern for all the monotheisms, the search for the Lost Speech, is a quest to recover the connection with the Angel, to cooperate in *being spoken* rather than simply speaking. The Angel is the empowering force and the North Star that orients the life of every believer. Corbin writes,

> This Angel endows the soul with the aptitude for thinking it and rising by it; he is the archetype, the finality without which a cause would never be a cause. He is the "destiny" of that soul... The act of thinking *is simultaneously* a being-thought by the Angel, causing the soul to be what he himself is.[8]

Living oriented by the Angel means that "every verb is mentally conjugated in the middle voice." The person is neither entirely autonomous and active, nor entirely passive and acted upon. Rather, she acts upon herself in such a way as to make herself *be* in the image of the archetypal Angel. Finding the middle voice is the key to recovering the Lost Speech. There is neither victimization of the individual by the impersonal forces of society, nor the blind abandonment

trans. Ralph Manheim (Princeton, N.J.: Princeton University Press, 1969). Reissued as *Alone with the Alone: Creative Imagination in the Sufism of Ibn 'Arabī* (Princeton, N.J.: Princeton University Press, 1997), 125.

8 "Cyclical Time in Mazdaism and Ismaili Gnosis," in Henry Corbin, *Cyclical Time and Ismaili Gnosis,* trans. Ralph Manheim and James W. Morris (London: Kegan Paul International, 1983), 52 (my italics).

of the person to an authoritarian Master. Finding the middle voice is a choice, a consciously chosen orientation, and a profoundly personal, intimate and individualizing stance towards the reality of the Angel. It is action of exquisitely sensitive response, and profound responsibility.

The notion was of particular importance to the poet Charles Olson who had by 1960 read Corbin's seminal essay. Olson's influence and his enthusiasm for Corbin's work are crucial elements in the dissemination of Corbin's ideas among American poets. Olson had encountered this particular idea several years earlier.[9] He got it from Stefan Wolpe, a pianist and composer who taught at Black Mountain College. Wolpe told him that the middle voice is "the thing that makes music work."[10] This is a perfect context for approaching Corbin's meaning, given how profoundly he thought and felt in musical terms. In 1961, Olson wrote a major poem, "Maximus, at the Harbor," which is shot through with references to Corbin's essay, in particular to what is perhaps the core of Corbin's spiritual phenomenology – the ontological significance of the middle voice in revealing the action of the Angel in us.[11]

Recovering the lost speech requires us to learn to listen. We need to locate that Angel. This requires a

9 The term first appears in Olson's "Tyrian Businesses," written in the spring of 1953. See Charles Olson and George F. Butterick, *The Maximus Poems* (Berkeley: University of California Press, 1983), *Maximus I*, 35-40. In May of 1961 Olson published "Grammar – a book" in *Floating Bear 7*, ed. Diane di Prima and LeRoi Jones, in which he further plays with notion of the "middle voice," so it was clearly still actively engaging his attention.

10 George F. Butterick, *A Guide to the Maximus Poems* (Berkeley: University of California Press, 1980), 59.

11 *Maximus II*, 70-71. See Ralph Maud, *Charles Olson at the Harbor* (Vancouver: Talon Books, 2008).

particular kind of attentiveness. But direct access is rare and is not under our control in any case. More often the Angel appears to us in our communication, our communion, with other people. We have to learn to listen to people. This is extremely hard. It means we have to become conscious of all the feeling-toned complexes that generally orchestrate the moods and experiences of our daily lives. We rarely really see or hear the people we meet – even those we are closest to. Perhaps even especially those we are closest to. What we see instead are what Jung called projections. Our own emotional reactions, moods and habitual patterns of feeling, thought and behavior obliterate the independent reality and the divine individuality of the other persons we encounter. Each of us lives in a world that is effectively one enormous spherical mirror, centered on ourselves. Once in a while something gets through, and it can be rather a shock.

So learning to listen means getting yourself out of the way. I know of no other way of doing this than becoming conscious of complexes. Jung said that confronting your darker nature, your shadow, was the apprentice piece of the process of becoming conscious. The confrontation with the deep unconscious, with the autonomous soul itself, the anima, is the masterpiece. James Hillman has pointed out that analytical psychology sometimes tends to confuse the functions of anima and feeling.[12] This is a disaster for human relations. The function of anima is to mediate unconsciousness.[13] It is largely the function of feeling to mediate relationship. But before human relations can be freed of the unconsciousness of complexes, the recognition of the unconsciousness in all our dealings with the

---

12 James Hillman, *Anima: An Anatomy of a Personified Notion* (Putnam, Conn.: Spring Publications, 2007), 39.

13 Ibid., 137.

world must be brought to light. So recognizing the actions of the anima comes before self-consciousness. As Hillman puts it, "soul-making precedes self-individuating. Soul-making in this context becomes nothing more than the rather humiliating recognition of the anima archetype."[14] We never become conscious of anima herself, for she is the archetype of unconsciousness. This means that recognition of her effects is the starting place for all psychic work and for the recognition of the all-embracing nature of psyche. Hillman says,

> The notion of unconsciousness means autonomous, spontaneous, ubiquitous, collective: it hits us ever again, popping up and spilling out smack in the middle of the market place. Each event that occurs in a day has an entropic, disintegrating effect. Each conversation, analytical hour, meditation, and dream, by moving consciousness, makes us unconscious in a new way. [Anima] mediates these shifts in unconsciousness.[15]

Anima connects us to the interiority of all our attachments, and the way in which she mediates is through images and the activities of the imagination. She leads us into ambiguity, unconsciousness, and unknowing. She connects us to the "primordial realm of the imaginal, its images, ideas, figures, and emotions."[16]

This is catastrophic for human relationships. Anima is the "bridge to everything unknown" and when anima is the archetype governing relationship then the autonomy and unconsciousness of the forces governing

---

14 Ibid.
15 Ibid., 137-39.
16 Ibid., 39.

the bond are stunning. "She makes moods, distortions, illusions," and is the greatest of all the disturbers of accurate feelings between persons. She produces an "intense sense of personal significance" and "swollen importance" that undermines the possibility of the feeling for the other that is necessary for the development of any real human relationship. As Hillman puts it: "If we want 'to relate,' then anima begone!"[17]

Now in cases of religious and political conflict it is surely true that there are sources besides the anima complex that distort and dominate human relations. But anima is the one I am most familiar with, and as she is the archetypal guide into the unconscious, she can be a central focus for coming to terms with the misunderstandings and the emotional energies that dominate so many human encounters.

Human relationships require constant negotiations of conflicts or potential conflicts, large and small and in-between. In order to make in progress in any situation of conflict you have to be able to imagine, feel, intuit, and think your way into the position of the other person. You have to be able to suspend your own viewpoint, and your own emotional reactions. Just as in alchemy – don't repress; don't act out: imagine. It is a handy shorthand to say you have to get rid of your *ego*. But the ego functions don't go: reality testing, impulse control, affect regulation, clarity of thought – these are all essential. What has to go is the overwhelming sense of personal significance that comes with anima, the profoundly inflated sense of the centrality of your own emotions that she brings. Hillman says, "In each of her classical shapes she is a nonhuman or half-human creature, and her effects lead us away from the individually

---

17 Ibid.

human situation."[18] She brings with her an experience of one's emotions as inhuman powers of nature – and a correspondingly profound unconsciousness that anything of the kind is going on. The power and autonomy of these all-consuming emotions makes them all but impossible to get outside of. They are not your emotions any more than the Atlantic is your ocean. One is decidedly "in" the complex – to the point that there simply *is* no other standpoint, and no possibility of objectivity. When she does eventually let you go, then you can ask, "What got into me?"

Coming to consciousness of the autonomy of the feeling-toned emotions that distort human relations is a long, hard slog. It is the opus itself. First, through the anima we recognize the psychic nature of all experience. Then we struggle with the passions over and over again. Gradually they become less autonomous, less powerful and dominant. The possibilities begin to open for other forms of relationship based not on impersonal passions but on our own individual, human feelings. This slow reformation of the personality is well described by the alchemical process of *solutio*.

There are no rules in alchemy – the texts we have from the tradition are as wild and chaotic as the work itself. But one command deserves particular attention here: Perform no operation until all has become water. Bonus of Ferraro said: "Solutio is the root of alchemy."[19] It is of special importance for counteracting the fixations and rigidities of monotheistic consciousness. One of the most enigmatic and important events in the Qur'an occurs, as we will see, in

---

18 Ibid.

19 Edward F. Edinger, *Anatomy of the Psyche: Alchemical Symbolism in Psychotherapy* (La Salle: Open Court, 1985), 48.

the unstable realm of mystery that exists at the confluence
between the inner world and the outer.

'Til All Become Water

In Sura XVIII, of the Qur'an, the figure who came to be
interpreted as Khidr, the Verdant One, or the Green
Man, appears in an strange, fragmented episode. Moses
and his servant travel to "the meeting place of the two
seas." There he meets an unnamed messenger. Henry
Corbin comments,

> He is represented as Moses' guide, who initi-
> ates Moses into "the science of predestination."
> Thus he reveals himself to be the repository of
> an inspired divine science, superior to the law
> (*shari'a*). Thus Khidr is superior to Moses in so
> far as Moses is a prophet invested with revealing
> a *shari'a*. He reveals to Moses the secret mys-
> tic truth...that transcends the *shari'a,* and this
> explains why the spirituality inaugurated by Khidr
> is free from the servitude of literal religion.[20]

The personal guide appears at the meeting place of the two
seas – in the middle realm between the outer world and the
inner. Corbin tells us that the function of this archetypal
person is

> to reveal each disciple to himself... He leads
> each disciple to his own theophany...because
> that theophany corresponds to his own "inner
> heaven," to the form of his own being, to his eter-
> nal individuality... Khidr's mission consists in

---

20 Corbin, *Creative Imagination,* 55.

enabling you to attain to the "Khidr of your being," for it is in this inner depth, in this "prophet of your being," that springs the Water of Life at the foot of the mystic Sinai, pole of the microcosm, center of the world.[21]

The middle realm that is the dwelling of the prophet of your being and the place of the fountain of life is a *barzakh,* an intermediate region at the margins between worlds. It is where the Water of Life can be found. Corbin tells us that you have to struggle to find it. It is the goal of the spiritual quest. He writes,

> Once the soul has emerged from Darkness, once it has risen from the abyss of unconsciousness, the first thing that presents itself is the living spring whose water flows out over the *barzakh*... For changing the appearance of things, walking on water, climbing [the mystic mountain]...[are all] psychic events whose scene and action are set in neither the sensible nor the intelligible worlds but in the intermediate world of the Imaginable, the *alam al-mithal,* as it is called, or the world of symbol and typifications, the *place* of all spiritual recitals. Now, this world is also called *barzakh* as interval extending between the intelligible and the sensible. It is the world in which spirits are corporealized and bodies spiritualized.[22]

William Chittick has explained Ibn 'Arabī's doctrine of the *barzakh* for us. How one thinks of the cosmos, or of anything

---

21 Ibid., 61.
22 Henry Corbin, *Avicenna and the Visionary Recital,* trans. Willard Trask (Princeton, N.J.: Princeton University Press, 1960), 161.

for that matter, depends on your perspective. As with many other Muslim thinkers, for Ibn 'Arabī spirit and body are not *things* but qualitative distinctions. The spiritual refers to that dimension that is luminous, alive, knowing, aware, and subtle. The bodily dimension lacks these things – it is dark, dead, unconscious, and heavy. The *intermediate* dimension of things, the dimension of the imagination and the soul is in between, neither wholly spiritual nor wholly material. Now while one can divide the cosmos into three realms, the lower corporeal, the intermediate imaginal and the higher spiritual, it is also true that all of existence is a *barzakh* between Being and Nothingness. And

> strictly speaking, every existing thing is a *barzakh,* since everything has a niche between two other niches within the ontological hierarchy known as the cosmos. [Ibn 'Arabī writes,] "There is nothing in existence but *barzakhs* since a *barzakh* is the arrangement of one thing between two things...and existence has no edges."[23]

All of Creation is the Imagination of God. But we are created in the image of God and our Imagination is distinct from but continuous with the divine source. Our perceptions of reality are always partial, always limited, but also always creative by virtue of our participation in the essential ambiguity of things. The entire cosmos exists in a perpetual state of ambiguity, both from God's point of view and from the vast multiplicities of human points of view. Understood from this point of view, which stresses ambiguity and creative flux, we feel that this ever-flowing creative spring is what we contact when we enter the realm of alchemy. We enter the deeps

---

23 William Chittick, *The Sufi Path of Knowledge: Ibn 'Arabī's Metaphysics of the Imagination* (Albany, N.Y.: SUNY Press, 1989), 14.

and are dissolved – that is a necessary part of the struggle to free ourselves from the passions and the compulsions of the fragments of persons we become when in the grip of unconscious complexes. Once we have begun to dissolve, we have taken the first steps on the road to the Fountain of Life. This dissolution of our dense and tightly held habits, reflexes, beliefs and ways of thought is the beginning of the cure for fundamentalism. In Henry Corbin's terms, fundamentalism is the single-minded adherence to a Truth that has become solidified and opaque. He tells us that

> idolatry consists in immobilizing oneself before an idol because one sees it as opaque, because one is incapable of discerning in it the hidden invitation that it offers to go beyond it. Hence, the opposite of idolatry would not consist in breaking idols, in practicing a fierce iconoclasm aimed against every inner or external Image; it would rather consist in rendering the idol transparent to the light invested in it. In short, it means transmuting the idol into an icon.[24]

Corbin favors metaphors of light. I favor those of water. There is much to ponder in the difference, but the phenomenologies of these elemental realities share many features. Chief among them perhaps are transparency and the transgression of boundaries. As an icon is a window lighted by the energies of the worlds beyond, so the waters that cool and disperse our fundamental passions has its source in the fountain at the meeting place of the two seas.

---

24   Henry Corbin, "Theophanies and Mirrors: Idols or Icons?," trans. Jane Pratt and A. K. Donohue, *Spring: An Annual of Archetypal Psychology and Jungian Thought* (1983), 2.

The Recurrent Creation

The centerpiece of Corbin's theology derives from Shi'ite Islam. The idea of *ta'wīl,* or spiritual hermeneutics is, he says, the central principle in *all* spiritual disciplines and "the mainspring of every spirituality... a procedure that engages the entire soul because it brings into play the soul's most secret sources of energy.[25] The practice of *ta'wīl* is how we recover the lost speech. Its mastery is the *magnum opus* of a lifetime. It is a discipline of "reading" and interpreting all things: a sacred text, the text of the world, and the soul itself as *metaphors* for the reality from which they derive. *Metaphor* means to "carry over," and the metaphoric vision of reality sees through the literal appearance to the Presence that lies behind the daylight Face of things. The *ta'wīl* is both a mode of perception and a mode of being. It is a way of seeing and a way of living that refuses the literal. It is how we can *live* the refusal of idolatry. It is the means by which idols are transmuted into icons. This spiritual unveiling

> consists in "bringing back," recalling, returning to its origin, not only the text of a book but also the cosmic context in which the soul is imprisoned. The soul must free this context, and free itself from it, by transmuting it into symbols.[26]

There are at least two steps involved in the "return to the origin." The "return" applies both to the *text* and the cosmic *context*. This vision of things assumes the all-encompassing embrace of language as a contextualizing of human experience. The *ta'wīl* requires that the literal appearance

---

25 Henry Corbin, *Avicenna and the Visionary Recital,* 28.
26 Ibid.

of all things be interpreted as *metaphor,* rather in the way we might view images in a dream. We are to be "carried over" somewhere. So, the sacred text and the world and the soul are first *deliteralized.* This serves to open the mind and the heart. It is a kind of "relativizing" move since in an alert but dreamlike state we are less apt to grasp for solid "facts."

The hard facts, fixed truths, and blind certainties of compulsion and fanaticism are melted by *solutio.* The deliteralization at the heart of *ta'wīl* likewise melts the world. The *ta'wīl* returns all things to their transcendent archetypes and in so doing dissolves time itself. The forward thrust of historical, linear Time from past through the present and on to future destroys creation by stopping it, fixing it, and making immutable past Fact from the infinite flux and potentiality of Creation. The metaphoric move of the *ta'wīl* is made possible by the cyclical time that flows from the idea of the recurrent creation in Islam. In a sense this bends linear time into a curve so that it returns back upon itself – but not only at the end of time as in mainstream Christian eschatology. Cyclical time undermines the thrust of time towards the future and so evades the catastrophe of history. All moments are contemporaneous – every instant all things participates in the Creation and the return to Paradise – Paradise is *now.* We are connected at each moment to the archetypal sources of our being – we are connected to the Angel of the Face at every instant. It is only a question of learning to know it.

In this sense then the linear time of historical consciousness is not absolute. And Islam does not conceive of time in the way that Western culture does. In his marvelous essay on Sura XVIII, Norman O. Brown puts it this way:

> The Qur'an backs off from that linear organiza-
> tion of time, revelation, and history which became
> the backbone of orthodox Christianity, and
> remains the backbone of Western culture after
> the death of God... In Sura XVIII, in the Qur'an,
> there is a mysterious regression to a more primi-
> tive stratum, archetypal, folkloristic, fabulous,
> apocryphal. Historical material is fragmented into
> its archetypal constituents, as in dreams... Islam
> is committed by the Qur'an to project a meta-
> historical plane on which the eternal meaning of
> historical events is disclosed... History *sub specie*
> *aeternitatis.*[27]

The past is not irrevocable. We are not in history, as Henry
Corbin says, history is in us. The past and the future,

> are not attributes of exterior things; they are
> attributes of the soul itself. It is we who are living
> or dead, and who are responsible for the life and
> death of these things.[28]

It is just possible that this view of human and divine life
might give hope to those who feel so entangled in the long
history of injustices, distrust and misunderstanding that
defines the modern Middle East that they accept the deter-
minations and inevitabilities of historical circumstance. For
Corbin it is the human soul that is ultimately the locus of
creativity and responsibility – ultimately free from the con-

---

27 "The Apocalypse of Islam," in Norman O. Brown, *Apocalypse
and/or Metamorphosis* (Berkeley: University of California Press,
1991), 86-88.
28 Henry Corbin, *En Islam iranien: aspects spirituels et philos-
ophiques I: Le shî'isme duodécemain* (Paris: Gallimard, 1971), 37.

straints and determinisms of an unalterable past. The past
is perpetually *unfinished*. Corbin says:

> If the past were really what we believe it to be,
> that is, completed and closed, it would not be
> the grounds of such vehement discussions... [A]
> ll our *acts of understanding* are so many recom-
> mencements, re-*iterations* of events still uncon-
> cluded... While we believe that we are looking
> at what is past and unchangeable, we are in fact
> consummating our own future... It follows that
> the whole of the underlying metaphysics is that of
> an unceasing recurrence of Creation; not a meta-
> physics of the *ens* and the *esse*, but of the *esto*, of
> being in the imperative. But the event is put, or put
> again, in the imperative only because it is itself the
> *iterative* form of *being* by which it is raised to the
> reality of an event.[29]

This vision of time as recurrent creation is incompatible
with fundamentalism that must always posit the fixed and
immutable passage of time. The past is Fact, the future is
threat of Hell or promise of Heaven—all of it defined, constricted, and fixed by acts that happen once and forever.

But here all our acts of understanding, of *ta'wīl*,
that is, of *being*, are reiterations of acts yet unconcluded,
perpetually in process of being raised to the reality of Event
by being conjugated over and over in the middle voice
whereby the solitary, isolated ego dies again and yet again so
that each time the Angel may resurrect us that we may *Be!*

---

29 Henry Corbin, *Spiritual Body and Celestial Earth: From Mazdean Iran to Shi'ite Iran,* trans. Nancy Pearson (Princeton, N.J.:
Princeton University Press, 1989), xxix.

in communion and released into the community of other persons.

Some events stand outside of historical time – they are made between and among persons, not figures in the flux of history. Perhaps Corbin is right that all real history is meta-history, occurring in eternal time. Perhaps it is the events that occur there that shape the course of the events we think of as real history. Then we can look for hope in the passionate, hopeful, trusting connections between individuals. These apparently insignificant events are perhaps indeed the only seeds of peace that ever have a real chance to grow.

4

The Boundaries of Imagination

Doctrines and Disciplines

When I was in graduate school in my early twenties I bought a copy of Wallace Stevens's *Collected Poems*. It was a required text for a philosophy course in the theory of knowledge. The professor was a wonderful man, Ernan McMullin, who was, and it seemed to me then rather odd, a Catholic priest, a theoretical physicist, and a respected philosopher of science. I didn't do very well in his course and never finished my degree in any case. I wasn't happy with my life, or with philosophy as I understood it. I didn't know that I was in the early stages of a long struggle to free myself from some dangerous fundamentalist traps that my attachment to philosophy only served to mask and strengthen. I wasn't a reader of poetry, or literature of any kind really, but the course intrigued me. Father McMullin was interested in the differences between the kind of knowledge that science provides and what happens to us when we read literature, which is in turn somehow related to the experience of reading a sacred text. He asked us to read Stevens's "big" poems: "The Idea of Order at Key West," "The Man with the Blue Guitar," and "Notes Towards a Supreme Fiction." Those were too much for me and didn't hold my attention, but a few of the shorter ones did. Two in particular did to me what poems are supposed to do: they changed something in me, if only for a moment – but I read them many times and my memory of the feeling of release they produced has stayed with me ever since. Here are a few lines from *On the Road Home*:

> It was when I said,
> "There is no such thing as the truth,"
> That the grapes seemed fatter.
> The fox ran out of his hole.

> You... You said,
> "There are many truths,
> But they are not parts of a truth."
> Then the tree, at night, began to change...[1]

"It was when I said,/"There is no such thing as the truth,"/ that the grapes seemed fatter./The fox ran out of his hole." When I first read these lines, and still today if I'm paying attention, this makes the muscles in my shoulders loosen and the world open up just a little bit. Listen to the beginning of the very next poem, on the facing page in my edition. It was, for me, a revelation. Here are some lines from the beginning of "The Latest Freed Man":

> Tired of the old descriptions of the world,
> The latest freed man rose at six and sat
> On the edge of his bed. He said,
>   "I suppose there is
> A doctrine to this landscape. Yet, having just
> Escaped from the truth, the morning is color and mist,
> Which is enough..."

> ... He bathes in the mist
> Like a man without a doctrine...[2]

---

1 *The Collected Poems of Wallace Stevens* (New York: Knopf, 1954), 204.
2 Ibid., 204-5.

I have wanted very much to be that freed man, a man without a doctrine. I have spent twenty years thinking about the
work of Henry Corbin, mystic, philosopher, and scholar of
Sufism. He shows how it is that doctrines and dogmas can
become rigid, opaque, and dangerous, how they hide the
world rather than reveal it – so that they kill the spirit and
suck the life out of the best of us. Then they are idols, and
we are idolators. The opposite of an idol is an icon, which
is transparent to the light and life of the world and always
leads beyond itself, opening into the plenitude and energy
that lie at the heart of the creation. But this is not an essay
on Corbin, though he will always be in the background. It is
a meditation on boundaries and the imagination, and how
we negotiate the doctrines and dogmas that, for the most
part unconsciously, rule our lives. Many of us live in little
ready-made boxes and never know it. Or if we do fall out,
sometimes we get scared and try to get back in. I'll tell you
a bit of my own story since it may sound familiar to some,
though few perhaps will have been in quite the same box.
It may sound "merely academic," but it didn't seem that
way to me.

Those many years ago reading Wallace Stevens
I began to sense that I needed to escape from something
that I thought at the time was "philosophy." I was looking
for truth of a sort that I thought it could provide. I had more
or less witlessly decided that the Germans had a monopoly
on profundity, because what I knew of their philosophiz-
ing seemed so deadly *serious*. Though I didn't know any
German, which now seems utterly scandalous to me, I had
become entangled in Hegel's metaphysics, had been struck
to the core by Nietzsche's claim to have seen the Abyss and
so understood the real nature of human life, and I wanted
to study Heidegger because he was notoriously difficult

and spent a lot of energy writing about Being and Resolve and Death. It took me a very long time to escape the gravitational pull of the ponderous weight and deadly seriousness that was killing me. All these years later, it seems to me that Hegel's astonishing system, impressive though it is, is a product of a stunning arrogance and presumption. And Henry Corbin taught me to see Nietzsche's vision of the Abyss as a failed initiation that the Sufi mystics understand full well as a principal danger of the mystic path. While finding much of importance in Heidegger, Corbin lightly dismisses his concern with Being-towards-death, saying that from the point of view of the spiritual masters of the religions of the Book, Heidegger had simply not seen the endless vistas that his own system opens up.

Corbin presents Heidegger's visionary conception of human being as a passageway towards immortality and transcendence. The Canadian poet Robert Bringhurst opens it to a view of language that is central to my purpose here. Much of Heidegger's work is devoted to thinking about language, particularly poetic language. For Heidegger, language gives us the ability to "think Being" and to be open to the mysteries of the world. And in fact Heidegger's later work is itself highly poetic. But Bringhurst finds his focus parochial, constricted, and blind to the plurality and diversity of actual languages in the world:

> Martin Heidegger claimed that our abilities with language give members of the species *Homo sapiens* privileged metaphysical status, but this merely repeats at a grander level the error Heidegger made when he claimed that the two languages most inherently disposed to speak the truth were

by coincidence two of the three or four languages he read, namely German and classical Greek.[3]

With this, Bringhurst throws open the shutters in a long-closed room to let in the warm light of day. And he has the credibility to say it: he is a polyglot who knows an impressive number of Western and non-Western languages including Arabic, as well as Haida and a few others spoken by the indigenous peoples of North America. He argues, persuasively to my mind, that Heidegger, like nearly all Western philosophers, has misunderstood the very nature of language. We need to think about it ecologically and biologically, not only anthropologically and philosophically. Bringhurst again:

> Like other creatures, humans are heavily self-absorbed. We frequently pretend...that language belongs to humans alone. And many of us claim that the only kind of human language, or the only kind that matters, is the kind that is born in the mouth. The languages of music and mathematics, the gestural languages of the deaf, the calls of leopard frogs and whales, the rituals of the mating sandhill cranes, and the chemical messages coming and going day and night within the brain itself are a few of the many reminders that language is actually part of the fire of which life is spun. We are able to think about language at all only because a license to do so is chemically written into our genes. The languages in which we are spoken are those for which we speak.[4]

3 Bringhurst, *The Tree of Meaning,* 128 (see chap. 2, n. 25).
4 Bringhurst, *The Solid Form of Language,* 10–11 (see chap. 2, n. 18).

This is a scientifically literate way to speak of the fact known to the masters and mystics of the great monotheisms that all creation is a kind of language.

To think this way breaks open the boundaries of thought and experience – it opens up the philosophical box I was trapped in for so long. Language is indeed central to human life and to the world in which we are embedded, but the particular language of philosophy can claim no special access to the Truth. No kind of language can. Many *bona fide* philosophers have argued just that. Richard Rorty, the American pragmatist, said simply that philosophy is a *genre of literature* invented by Plato.[5] It is a way of thinking and writing and speaking. And Ludwig Wittgenstein thought that "philosophy ought really to be written only as a *poetic composition.*"[6] Accepting this doesn't compromise the seriousness and rigor of thought, but it opens it to a wider and more creative life. And it does let the sun and the fresh air into the room. Realizing that philosophy is a genre of literature invented in ancient Greece dissolves the heavy mass that philosophy had become for me and reveals it as akin to myth, poetry, and song. That is the context out of which it arose in the works of Plato where these connections are still evident. For me this had the same liberating effect as James Hillman's work shifting the imagination of psychology from the northern European imaginations of Freud, Jung and Adler towards the south where we can breathe the Mediterranean air with Heraclitus, Plato, Ploti-

5 Richard Rorty, *Consequences of Pragmatism: Essays, 1972-1980* (Minneapolis: University of Minnesota Press, 1982), xiv.
6 Ludwig Wittgenstein, *Culture and Value,* ed. G.H. von Wright, trans. P. Winch (Chicago: The University of Chicago Press, 1980), 24.

110

nus, Vico, and Ficino. In fairness to Heidegger, this may well be the kind of thing he was after, really.

The Boundaries of Consciousness

I t is not just philosophical writing that is a genre of litera-ture. All writing is. There is no clear distinction between the literal and the fictive. The real relation between language and the world is much more complex. What we have instead are styles of imagining and genres of thinking and writing. That includes science itself—which is, along with fundamentalist religion, one of the bastions of literalism in our time. What is crucial for any humane life is an ability to move among these styles in accordance with your desires and intentions and the demands of the world hand. In order to do that, there has to be a space, a cosmos, in which all these styles coexist and in which you can learn to move with some assurance. There is only one world big enough: the world of what Corbin called the creative imagination, and that we might call the world of the fictive. Here imagination lies at the center of reality. In my experience, it is literature, poetry in particular, that can sensitize us to the changes in consciousness that the movements between these various styles of thought, sensation and mood require.

We cross into different spaces all the time, but mostly we don't notice. Even the most normal day is a journey through multiple "spaces" in each of which we and the world we inhabit are just slightly different. We behave differently, we sense differently—our *being* is different. When we recognize this variety at all we speak of "moods" and "perspectives" and "attitudes." That language enshrines a dualistic view of the world in which there is a unitary subject moving around in a three-dimensional space filled with objects. If we imagine the subtly changing reality more precisely, then our experience of it will be more alive, we will be more aware of the field of phenomena. We will be less like passive objects and more like persons engaged in making and living in a world.

How do we speak of these things? What vocabulary can best help us see where we want to go? If talking about moods and attitudes and emotions gets things wrong, then how do we more usefully speak of what is going on? I am very drawn to the rich metaphors of biology, especially ecology, but these need to be embedded in a context broader than the one natural science provides. After long puzzling over this, it seems I am stuck doing what Hillman and many others have done: co-opting Henry Corbin's language – in particular his idea of the Imaginal, which he in turn had adapted from the writings of his Islamic masters. In fact I have been doing it for a long time, but I'm still slightly reluctant to admit it since it would have made Corbin very upset. He wanted to restrict the notion to very specific realms of spiritual, and indeed mystical reality. But I can't do that because I need the concept, the objective reality of which he defends so powerfully, in order to emphasize the *continuity* of everydayness with the mystical. There are ruptures, gulfs, chasms that divide certain aspects of religious experience from washing dishes, changing diapers, planting tomatoes, and driving to work. No doubt. But we have to have some way of speaking of the connections unless we are to give up any attempt to make sense of the unity of human experience – what Robert Duncan called the "symposium of the whole." And Corbin's term "imaginal" serves that purpose. It evokes a realm that is not anchored in the ego or in things, but wholly open to the full range and variety of experience – I would say, to the Imagination. It serves as a "field concept" in both the scientific sense and Duncan's sense of an opened field, a meadow, a "made place, near to the heart." In order to appreciate our lived experience as occurring in an imaginal realm at all we have to cultivate, as Hillman says, imaginal sensibilities. We have to understand the fundamentally "poetic" basis of experience and tune our poetic sensibilities. In philosophical terms, if we need them, this is quite like the practice of phenomenology. A phenomenological attitude serves to open us to *all* experience. We try to suspend all our our preconceptions of what is important and what counts as real. Everything is real; and we don't know what is important. It's extremely hard – paying attention to everything. We can't actually do it – reality is too rich. Experience never comes raw anyway – it's always "cooked," though the cuisines are various. The notion of a world "out there" independent of any experiencing subject "in here" is nonsense. That's just the dualistic scheme again setting a subject up against objects. We've done away with that by acknowledging that what there is instead is an imaginal field where phenomena unfold.

So let's think about one particularly fruitful style of cooking experience. We have it thanks to C.G. Jung. To understand it we have to obliterate a distinction that I think is common, pernicious, and unacknowledged. Now the notion of an imaginal realm suggests boundlessness and spiritual freedom. Corbin certainly meant to imply this. But it does not signify "boundary-less-ness" or *unconstrained* freedom. One of the delusions that I have had a hard time banishing from my own mind is the notion that there is some clear distinction between the free play of fantasy in the "inner" world of imagination and the rock-solid constraints of a "literal," public world. This may come from my parents mostly, but I think it is also embedded in the culture

I grew up in. But in the cosmos we are discovering here, that scheme dissolves. The imaginal realm in which the so-called literal world *and* the worlds of fantasy, psychology, art, and fiction all have their place is replete with constraints, boundaries, discontinuities, blockages, walls, and difficult realities of too many kinds to count. This should I suppose be obvious, but it took me a long time to learn. Anyone with any psychological sophistication will know what I mean. Two examples: Now and then over the years I have stumbled and fallen – off a ladder or into a hole. You will know the feeling: a panicked moment of free fall, disorientation, and helplessness. I have also fallen into another kind of pit a few times. When confronted by the anger of a woman, I am completely undone. I go blank and come apart inside, utterly at a loss and powerless to respond with anything but a numb stare. Or again – I have twice in my life been bitten by a dog. These attacks came out of nowhere, were frightening and destructive. And I have, I am sorry to say, myself erupted in rage at another person. Also twice, actually. And they were both big men too . . . My inner hound was just as objective as the canines that bit me and my inarticulate incapacity to respond to a woman's anger just as real and empty as an open pit.

Jung had a way of thinking about these episodes of unconsciousness that is extremely useful. His approach was to reanimate the ancient and difficult art of slow cooking, the art of alchemy. He began by providing us with the notion of the "feeling-toned complex." Jung recognized lots of complexes and came to divide psychic reality up into archetypal regions to correspond, more or less, to them. Each has a characteristic style and emotional atmosphere, and each expresses some part of a complete personality – they are "partial personalities" Jung says. They correspond to styles of behavior, ways of experiencing, and even modes of being. And we are always in one complex or another – or let's say one or another is generally dominant at any given moment. And that doesn't necessarily suggest pathology – we're always in some mode of consciousness. James Hillman has usefully suggested that the Greek pantheon of gods and goddesses is another way of understanding the archetypal dominants that we naturally inhabit. This reminds us that there are lots of emotional atmospheres and styles of experience, mirroring the diversity of organisms and ecosystems in the biological world. Archetypes of one brand or another help to map our experience and our behavior. When a woman is angry, I fall into the hell of the Dark Mother. When I am in a rage, I am in the grip of Mars. This kind of analysis can of course be applied routinely and become just another system. I am not very interested in putting a label on modes of experience. That can do more harm than good. Having a map that is too detailed removes the immediacy of personal experience. Knowing *that* you are under some influence the ego has little or no control over is the first challenge. And it seems to me that is pretty rare. To acknowledge that I am always under the influence of some complex or other is extremely helpful in making it through the day. It doesn't absolve you of responsibility; on the contrary, it helps you pay attention and know what is going on. The ego is not master in its own house. It is good to remember this.

But how do we recognize we are in a complex? Extreme emotions are good place to start. They are starkly different from normal moods, and are generally over fairly quickly. Sudden and intense – so we say "Wow! What got into me?!" The boundaries in time, intensity, and mood are obvious. This is useful because the only way we know we are somewhere *at all* is by discovering that we are not somewhere else. That is the chief importance of boundaries. The only way we know where we are is because of the experience of crossing boundaries. No boundary crossing, no consciousness. When a boundary is crossed, something is suddenly different – an awareness dawns where before there was none. Berrigan reads Scalapino and remembers, "oh! right! that was where I wanted to be! I forgot!" Primordially, the newborn baby has to find out that there is a difference between her body and her mother's. That is the first boundary we all encounter and it produces the first consciousness – the ego complex. The long, slow process of becoming conscious of a complex that has you in its grasp is based on the repeated crossing of such a boundary. *Every* time you have strong emotions you are in the grip of a complex. I learned this from Jung, but most clearly and distinctly from Edward Whitmont's fine book *The Symbolic Quest*.[7] I had to read that part over and over for many unconscious years until I finally really got it.

Why does it take so long? Because the complex is unconscious: void, blank, an *unknown* unknown. The experience of it is shapeless, fleeting, vague, undefined. As Jung said, you can't understand anything psychological unless you have experienced it yourself, and the experience of unconsciousness that being in the grasp of a complex involves is particularly difficult to describe. But becoming conscious of a complex does involve the recognition of the boundary crossing that occurs as you pass into and out of its influence. It takes many, many crossings, that are only very slowly noticed as such. Only slowly does memory take hold and the experience itself start to take shape. Where before there was

7 Edward C. Whitmont, *The Symbolic Quest: Basic Concepts of Analytical Psychology* (Princeton, N.J.: Princeton University Press, 1991).

only chaos, pain, confusion, possession—all so impossible to articulate that it barely stays in the memory—gradually the fact of the transition, the border, becomes clearer and an experience begins to form where before there was none. Even this confused description overstates the clarity of the situation, and no doubt there are nearly infinite variations on the theme. But something has to take shape for consciousness to develop. You have to get an image. Of course, an image is not a picture—it may have little or no visual component, and manifests as a psychosomatic *event*. Perhaps it is better to say that something has to become present. And presence is always presence *to* consciousness. So, something appears, and it is recognized as Other. And the difference between self and other derives from crossing a border that is finally recognized as a border.

This spatial metaphor is important since it highlights the fact that the partial personality of the complex is also at the same time, a *place,* a landscape and topography. In the world experienced imaginally, persons *are* places and places are personalities—both are manifestations of the same Presence. Henry Corbin says "What would a world without a Face actually be?" It would be nothing—it would not be present at all. By uniting Face and Place, Corbin reveals a cosmology in which there is no schism between the inner and the outer, the psychological and the natural worlds. Coming to consciousness always knits parts of the world together. And in the normal course of things, as the complex becomes more conscious, more defined, and more present, it becomes less difficult to manage, less extreme, less destructive. The raging storm subsides. But the therapeutic task of confronting a complex does not mean we have to banish all strong emotions. You have to keep the heat up to do this slow cooking. Though we all need to learn that whenever our emotional temperature rises we had better beware: we are crossing over into another psyche and the world of feeling that is its home.

The great German poet Rainer Maria Rilke was suspicious of psychoanalysis. In 1912, he wrote in a letter to a friend that he would not enter analysis, fearing that if his devils were to leave him, the angels would too.[8] I share his wariness – not about depth psychology, which probably saved my life, but about its aims. I'm not looking to eliminate any demons, just to learn something of their taxonomy, their behavior and natural history. Rilke was far too sensitive to think that the imaginal world is neatly divided into angelic and demonic powers. That is another destructive dualism. When *we* are insensitive and unconscious, then we see the world as black and white – full of fundamentalist angels and demons. The more conscious and sensitive you become, the more complex and interesting the world and its inhabitants becomes – and the less likely the constellated complexes are to manifest as terrorists. What you need to begin with is some working knowledge of the beings whose project seems to be to torment you, so that you can find out what is it that they want. Then the effects of the distress they cause won't radiate outward and engulf everyone around you. In the beginning of this long process it seems there is to be no escape from the pure and demonic energies of the complexes, but you can learn, with considerable effort, to stand slightly aside while they engulf and move through you. Then you can learn to *see* them instead of *be* them.

---

8 Letter to Baron Emil von Gebsattel, 24 January 1912, in *Selected Letters of Rainer Maria Rilke,* trans R.F.C. Hull (London: Macmillan, 1946).

That is what the ascetics of the early Christian church called *apatheia,* and the achievement of that state of grace is the primary requirement to be met before you can begin let the fecundity of the world unfold in all its variety and wonder. You need to be able to let the energies of life flow through you, aware and conscious, and not live always at the mercy of those great powers.

The world unfolds itself and differentiates naturally – this is one of the laws of biology. It is also one of the laws of Creation and descent as understood in the psycho-cosmology of Henry Corbin and Ibn ʿArabī. If you try to fight it, all hell will break lose. Organisms appear to fill every available niche, and simplicity is an unstable state. Diversification is the normal, healthy process of ecological development. We need to understand this to be as true of psychic life as it is of organic life. For we are indeed, as Jung taught us, "always in psyche." The poet and naturalist Gary Snyder has had this right for a long time. He said: "It is in the deep mind that wilderness and the unconscious become one, and in some half-understood but very profound way, our relation to the outer ecologies seems conditioned by our inner ecologies. This is a metaphor, but it is also literal."[9] We need to conceive of the psyche ecologically in order to fully appreciate the wisdom of "psycho-diversity" and to make it possible for us to experience and value the richness and fecundity of the world. Hillman called this a "polytheism of consciousness" in contrast to the monotheism of consciousness that has permeated Western thought and culture for centuries. The tighter we hold to the unified

---

9 Gary Snyder, quoted in the introduction to Clayton Eshleman, *Juniper Fuse: Upper Paleolithic Imagination & the Construction of the Underworld* (Middletown, Conn.: Wesleyan University Press, 2003).

and defensive posings of the ego complex, the less able we are to see the diversities of the natural and human worlds in which we move and breathe, and of the presences and figures who move and breathe in us. From the point of view of the psychologies of Jung and Hillman this means we have to develop a fully alchemical view of ecology and an ecological understanding of alchemy so that each informs and enriches the other. Doing so breaks down the barriers that have separated the inner and the outer, the psyche and nature, the subjective and the objective and have caused the fundamental misunderstandings of our place in the world that have plagued Western consciousness for centuries.

In *Psychological Types*, Jung remarks on the "thing-like-ness" of "primitive thought." His sense of the "substance" of the psyche derives of course from his own alchemical journey, and like most people of his time he thought of the nonrational aspects of human life as "primitive." But we can abandon the connotations of the archaic and the primitive in favor of metaphors of open-ness. There is nothing particularly "primitive" about the substance of thought, though it has often been obliterated by historically late developments in human culture. Recall the history of consciousness in Western Europe as recounted by Cranz in Chapter 2. He argued that before the eleventh century, more or less, people in the Western world—the Greeks, the Romans and the Greco-Roman Christians in particular—had a very different experience of the world than that which was about to arise. They had an "extensive self" as opposed to the "intensive self" that has been dominant in the West ever since. He correlated this turn with the rise, among other things, of an exclusively "human-centered" understanding of language, that experiences language and thought as composed of *human* meanings. This jambs us inside our heads and gave rise to the Cartesian view of the mind and all the dualisms that come with it. An experience of the extensive self on the other hand is wide open to the world. The premoderns

> experienced an awareness open to what lay around them, and they experienced no sense of dichotomy between their awareness and everything else. What they found in their own minds or intellects was of like character with much of what was outside it; what they found in the world could in large part move directly into their minds and be possessed by it. There was an *ontological continuity* between what happened in their intellects and what happened in the kosmos or world.

There was no profound difference between thoughts and things, and so, no schism between the psyche and the cosmos. A phrase from anthropologist Claude Lévi-Strauss is helpful here. He wrote in his 1962 book *The Savage Mind* that "primitive" people had totem animals because plants and animals are "good to think with." The larger point is that things in general are good to think with. I think it is clear that artists do their work by thinking with things. This is particularly clear in the case of sculpture and architecture but applies across the board to all the arts. Dancers think and speak with their bodies. Painters think with paint. And the kind of thinking that is done with things is the kind of thinking that is done in alchemy. James Elkins makes this point in great detail in his book *What Painting Is*.[10] Elkins is very critical of Jung's approach to alchemy in

---

10 James Elkins, *What Painting Is: How to Think About Oil Painting, Using the Language of Alchemy* (New York: Routledge, 1999).

large part because Jung, he says, made alchemy an entirely spiritual pursuit independent of the laboratory. But he gets this wrong. Jung knew full well that spiritual alchemy is intensely somatic, and his development of the technique of active imagination is based fundamentally on working with images in *matter*—in stone and in paint in Jung's own case, but also of course in dance and in sandplay and other techniques developed by Jung's followers. And this includes, crucially, the embodied, material forms of language in the calligraphies of the *Red Book,* in stone sculpture, and in the *spoken* word that is so central to therapeutic technique. I think that we need to come to understand that the distinction between spiritual alchemy and what happens in art of all kinds, including the arts of language, is not very great. In order to re-establish something like an intensive self and experience the ontological continuity between thought and things we have to have an alchemical view of reality. The so-called inner world is continuous with the outer. Ideas are not in the head—they are in the world. They change the thinker and they change the world. Emotions are not private—they spill out all around us and manifest in our behavior and our relations with other people. Ideas and emotions are aspects of the feeling-toned complexes that Jung recognized to be "partial personalities" and they have bodies, both coarse and subtle, that extend into the world around us. This is why Walt Whitman could exult that "I contain multitudes." These multitudes are in perfect accord with the multitudes who inhabit the world known to the naturalist and why we must speak of a natural history of the psyche. All the dualisms fragment like this and the world explodes in diversity.

One of the simple dichotomies that breaks down to release the wild variety of life is that between the

demons and the angels. The very fact that there are hierarchies of angels described in the theologies of the prophetic
tradition suggests that we develop a more complex and
interesting taxonomy of the imaginal realm in which they
exist. Recall Rilke's fear that if his demons were to disappear it might frighten off his angels as well. The world of his
poetry is hardly limited to those two embattled species – it
is resplendent with presences of every sort. One of his short
poems gives us an image of an intermediate, imaginal world
flooded with the plenitude of presences and energies that
fill the spaces between the angelic and the demonic. It is
called *Moving Forward*:

> The deep parts of my life pour onward,
> as if the river shores were opening out.
> It seems that things are more like me now,
> that I can see farther into paintings.
> I feel closer to what language can't reach.
> With my senses, as with birds, I climb
> into the windy heaven, out of the oak,
> and in the ponds broken off from the sky
> my feeling sinks, as if standing on fishes.[11]

Here the cosmos is alive with wind and trees and water,
with birds and fishes. This is the primary poetry of the
world–before it breaks up into the inner and the outer, the
psychological and the biological. This is the primordial phenomenology of life. Listen to Walt Whitman discovering with
astonishment and joy that he is a microcosm of all Creation:

> I believe a leaf of grass is no less than the journey
>   work of the stars,

---

11 From Rilke's *Book of Images,* in *Selected Poems of Rainer Maria
Rilke,* trans. Robert Bly (New York: Harper & Row, 1981), 101.

And the pismire is equally perfect, and a grain of
    sand, and the egg of the wren,
And the tree-toad is a chef-d'oeuvre for the highest,
And the running blackberry would adorn the parlors
    of heaven,
And the narrowest hinge in my hand puts to scorn
    all machinery,
And the cow crunching with depress'd head
    surpasses any statue,
And a mouse is miracle enough to stagger sextillions
    of infidels.

I find I incorporate gneiss, coal, long-threaded moss,
    fruits, grains, esculent roots,
And am stucco'd with quadrupeds and birds
    all over... [12]

The poets are not giving us an account of the world of the strictly scientific naturalist, but of a cosmos much larger and even more charged with life. They invoke the presences of a creation that does not privilege the boundary between the inner and the outer, the subjective and the objective. They are the primary naturalists, moving with awe and wonder in the landscapes of a stunning New World like von Humboldt and Darwin in the Americas. Listen to a few lines by Pablo Neruda describing "Some Beasts" whose presence we feel with stunning immediacy:

It was the twilight of the iguana [...]

The jaguar touches the leaves
with its phosphorescent absence,

---

12 Walt Whitman, *Leaves of Grass: Authoritative Texts, Prefaces, Whitman on His Art, Criticism,* ed. Sculley Beadley and Haraold William Blodgett (New York: Norton, 1973), 59.

the puma bolts through the foliage
like a raging fire,
while in him burn
the jungle's alcoholic eyes.

And in the depths of the almighty water
lies the giant anaconda
like the circle of the earth,
covered with ritual clays,
devouring and religious.[13]

The force of such imagery depends on our ability to open the gates of the ego and come into the presence of these other beings who live as much within us as in the jungles of the tropics. The Swedish poet and Nobel laureate Tomas Tranströmer has a fine image for what happens in the absence of such an "imaginal sensibility." Here an artist loses contact with the living force of creation:

An artist said: Before I was a planet
With its own dense atmosphere.
Entering rays were broken into rainbows.
Perpetual raging thunderstorms, within.

Now I'm extinct and dry and open.
I no longer have child-like energy.
I have a hot side and a cold side.

No rainbows.[14]

---

13 Pablo Neruda, *Canto General,* trans. Jack Schmidt (Berkeley: University of California Press, 1991), 16-17.

14 "The Gallery," in Tomas Tranströmer, *The Great Enigma: New Collected Poems,* trans. Robin Fulton (New York: New Directions, 2006), 153.

Anyone with only a hot side and a cold side will live in a world polarized into radical angels and demons. The tensions are dangerous and appalling.

And notice that the artist is the whole planet – dense atmosphere, forests, storms and rainbows – and is full of childlike energies. That is a beautiful image of what living out of imagination can be like. But you can become extinct like a dead volcano by losing contact with imagination and being transformed into a dualist inhabiting the simple world of a literalist, a fundamentalist. All the creatures in your world will go extinct too. But on the other hand when you are fully alive to the energies of the world, you want to be, as Tranströmer suggests, the *whole planet* and not simply identify with the energies. You don't want to *be* those raging thunderstorms. That is very dangerous. But you do want to experience them. In order to experience them you in fact *cannot* be them. Thunderstorms don't know they are thunderstorms – they just rage. You cannot experience the storm unless you know you are in one. And you can't know you are in one unless you are conscious of the boundary, the separation, between you and the storm. The storms don't see the rainbows, they just rage on.

Just as important as the storms that rage are the smaller, more subtle and furtive energies. These are personalities, partial and otherwise – they are the creatures of our worlds. James Hillman presented the wide range of Greek gods as providing a far better language, a better taxonomy for the psyche than monotheism ever could. I have found this useful but always thought that the world of biology, and natural science in general, might provide an even better range of languages. Hillman knew this too and his writings on animal presence in which he often draws on the work of his Eranos colleague, the biologist Adolf Portmann, are to

me among the most significant part of his opus. The poetry
of the world in every language is so full of animals it is really
quite astounding. Recall Stevens's fox who ran out of his
hole, and the great ox of the latest freed man. Even Wallace Stevens is full of wild animal consciousnesses – though
they are from a wilderness as imagined by a vice president
of the Hartford Accident and Indemnity Company. Monotheism is a kind of monoculture, and any ecologist will tell
you that is an unsustainable system. We need all the creatures to give consciousness to the world. I am more than
willing to give consciousness to plants, and like Charles
Simic, to stones too. When we conceive of consciousness
as a strange magic that happens only in our human heads it
sucks the life out of everything else in existence.

I have been thinking lately about the European invasion
and colonization of the Americas. It was an apocalypse of
unimaginable scale. But it was part of an even larger story of
a great monoculture of consciousness spreading through
the Western world. In 1492, Columbus landed in the New
World and the Moors were finally expelled from Granada
in the last victory of the Reconquista. The Muslims were
driven out; shortly the Jews were driven out; the Inquisition
was not long away. Where all three of the great monotheisms had coexisted side by side in peace, however uneasy
it may have been, with the final dominion of the One True
Church all that came to an end. No more Ibn 'Arabīs would
be born in Murcia. No more Abraham Abulafias in Zara-
goza. The poet H.D., in speaking of her fear that we would
lose the kind of mystical consciousness from which her
poetry derives, said simply: "What can be seen is at stake."
Monotheistic consciousness risks a horrifying constriction

of reality and of empathy. The colonizers cannot see the colonized. It is a supreme example of what William Blake called Single Vision, and it is violent and destructive beyond imagining. It is no coincidence that the most perceptive Europeans to visit the New World were naturalists like von Humboldt and Darwin. There is some profound homology in the lives of poets, artists, mystics, and naturalists. All are boundary crossers with a deep sense of the integrity of all the beings that inhabit Creation. All are willing to risk everything in order to be open to the world.

Walking Off the Map

Becoming conscious of a complex requires the repeated crossing of the boundaries of consciousness. This can be frightening and disorienting, like stepping into a void. But eventually some being will take shape so that you can see it. In my own life, at the pivotal moment of my greatest and longest trial, the being that came to me was something like a bear. I say "something like a bear" because what I experienced was a bear-like presence—but it remained dim and dreamlike, simultaneously arising from and receding into shadow. That is how every real being comes to us. Only abstractions are known whole—reality is always more than we can know. This is what keeps the world open and us free. As an epigraph to his poem "To the Unseen Animal" Wendell Berry gives us a quote from his young daughter: "I hope there's an animal somewhere that nobody has ever seen. And I hope nobody ever sees it." That is why so many people are so passionate about preserving wilderness. We need it if we are to be free. We need to know that we can still walk off the edges of the map.

It seems to me that one of the potential dangers of studying Henry Corbin, or any of the mystics, is that they can make us want too much. I am perhaps fortunate to have always been slightly wary of Corbin's tendency towards other-worldliness. Not that I am unattracted by transcendence. This world is shot through with horror and evil and anyone who doesn't sometimes long to escape is simply not paying attention. But what is so very valuable in Corbin's work as I have read it is his insistence on the realities of the *inter-mediate* realm – the *mundus imaginalis,* the imaginal world, between the material and the spiritual. It is, I think, the world of immanence as *dependent* on transcendence. What William James, the great psychologist and philosopher would have called the "cash value" of the idea is this: it awakens us to the extraordinary richness and subtlety of immediate experience. The function of transcendence is to make immanence liquid, like light. Corbin said all the world is one vast iconostasis – all the world is an icon. To understand this you cannot live in a world of abstractions and abstractedness. We all do, most of the time. But now and then we really pay attention and something subtle happens.

Last fall I was walking in the field behind our house. We cleared it from the forest some years ago. I needed to get a bit of exercise so I planned on making several circuits around the edges of the clearing. I've walked there count-less times but hadn't in some weeks so the details of the vegetation were all new, and as I made my first circuit I watched my steps quite closely, seeing the shoots and the saplings and the insects and the moss and lichens on the tree stumps. There is lots of life in such a place. As I com-pleted the first lap I saw that I had left a trail for myself and I could see just where I had placed each footstep in the damp ground. Unthinking, I followed myself, like Pooh and Piglet pursuing Heffalumps. Immediately my attention wandered and my mind was in some other place. I had a map—a marked trail—and I didn't need to pay attention anymore. Now there is much to be said about the virtues of maps—and in this case perhaps I had a good idea or two while my mind wandered off. But it is so important to be able to notice the difference. In each case my imagination was fully engaged, but with different things. But it struck me quite forcibly that with each circuit of my trail I was seeing less and less of what was there and I was less and less actively engaged in my own immediate actions. Making a trail is a far different experience than following one. Of course this is what mystics are always up to—making new paths into spiritual worlds, rather than following the paths laid down by orthodoxy and tradition. If we live too much reading the maps others have made, or that we have made for ourselves, then we will miss the extraordinary fecundity, beauty and detail of the world. The poets and the naturalists move so slowly—at the limits of attention to the iconic details of the world we are slowed in stunned amazement. This is one reason poets and mystics make such bad politicians—to do anything at all with the world you have to see it abstractly. The full reality of things is far too complex for any response beyond simply standing there and singing.

As I made my way around my little trail, I was struck with a sudden deep sense of how much of my life I have spent inside various boxes, trying, mostly unconsciously, to get out. That is why Wallace Stevens meant so much to me those many years ago.

Coda: In Praise of the Imaginal

I want to close with an homage to James Hillman, whose work probably literally saved my life and without whom I never would have known about Henry Corbin. I found Hillman's own homage to Corbin so thrilling that I immediately bought Corbin's book on Ibn 'Arabī. In *The Thought of the Heart and the Soul of the World,* Hillman says:

> You who have been privileged at some time during his long life to have attended a lecture by Henry Corbin have been present at a manifestation of the thought of the heart. You have been witness to its creative imagination, its theophanic power of bringing the divine face into visibility. You will also know in your hearts that the communication of the thought of the heart proceeds in that fashion of which he was master, as a *récit,* an account of the imaginal life as a journey among imaginal essences, an account of the essential. In him, imagination was utterly presence. One was in presence of imagination itself, that imagination in which and by which the spirit moves from the heart toward all origination.[15]

It was to be many years before I came to understand the transformational power of imagination and of poetry, though I had suspected it all my life. And it was later yet before I understood how it is that the imagination bridges the gap between matter and mind, the animal and the spiritual, that has caused such damage over the course of Western history. Hillman continues,

---

15   James Hillman, *The Thought of the Heart and the Soul of the World* (Putnam, Conn.: Spring Publications, 2014), 9.

[Those of you who have attended a lecture by Corbin]...have already seen and heard the themes that I shall be attempting...as they were embodied in the physical intensity of that living man, Henry Corbin: the thought of the heart as sovereign and noble, as joyous, as subtle as an animal, bold, courageous and encouraging, as delighting in intellectual forms and fierce in their defense, ever-extending equally in its compassion and in its visionary power, forming a beauty in the language of images.

We need to take these words as a call to action. We, too, need to be courageous and fierce in the defense of the imagination against every form of fundamentalism. We, too, need to be subtle as animals and visionary at the same time since the visionary is supremely subtle and always embodied. Henry Corbin was engaged all his life in what he called the battle for the soul of the world. It is a battle we avoid at our peril. The poet Diane di Prima wrote to me once and confirmed that Corbin's work was simply part of the atmosphere among poets in the 1960s and 1970s.

THE ONLY WAR THAT MATTERS IS THE WAR
AGAINST THE IMAGINATION

ALL OTHER WARS ARE SUBSUMED IN IT

[...]

the war is the war for the human imagination
and no one can fight it but you/ & no one can fight it
for you.[16]

---

16 Diane di Prima, "Rant," in *Poems for the Millennium,* Vol. 2: From Postwar to Millennium, ed. Jerome Rothenberg and Pierre Joris (Berkeley: University of California Press, 1998), 449-50.

5

Concrete Imagination

Where the Wild Things Are

When I was in grade school I had a "natural-history museum" in my bedroom. But that wasn't nearly enough space, and it spilled over into the large adjoining playroom. Wooden crates and cardboard boxes lined the walls, and every available surface was devoted to the display of my treasures. I had bones and antlers, rocks and minerals, arrowheads and insects, mosses and lichens, and jars full of alcohol-preserved organs we got from the local butcher, and terraria and aquaria with fish and frogs and worms and turtles wandering around inside. In one memorable episode the praying mantis egg case I had kept for months burst open overnight and thousands of tiny hatchlings were swarming out over my dresser in the morning. I don't remember when I dismantled it all. I do know that later on my room was filled with books and the walls were covered in maps. I love books and the worlds they open and I am mesmerized by the deep magic of maps, but I think now that I have spent a lot of time over the years trying to get that other lively, chaotic wilderness back inside my house.

Sometime during my early life as a naturalist I came upon a quote from the biologist J.B.S. Haldane that has been rattling around in the back of my head ever since. He wrote, "I have no doubt that in reality the future will be vastly more surprising than anything I can imagine. Now my own suspicion is that the Universe is not only queerer than we suppose, but queerer than we *can* suppose."[1] Trying to learn to take this seriously seems to have been something of a life's work for me. I didn't know that was what was going on and I went about things in a very haphazard way. I think that I have long assumed that the queerness of the world depends upon its inexhaustible richness and diversity. To have a sense of this wildness you have to look at things from a lot of very different and seemingly unrelated perspectives. I have done that over the years and it has been interesting. My life has had several chapters with roughly this arc: something about the world would grab my attention, and I would spend much time and no little intensity exploring. At some point along the way, unpredictably, the flame would die away, my vision would dim, and the world recede back into greyness. And then, I would wait for the next spark to burst into flame. It has proven hard to stay continuously open to the fountain of weirdness at the heart of reality. I would like to know how to do that.

My mother said of one of my early shorter-lived enthusiasms, "Well, that was a flash-in-the-pan." Perhaps a little more encouragement might have been good for me, but maybe that image of that flash was a real gift. I know the light and the heat it gives. But what is the source of the fire? Is it possible to learn to make our own sparks? I used to encourage my students to try to generate some "imaginative interaction" with whatever subject matter I was trying to help them learn. But it isn't necessarily easy. How do we get energized? Does it have to come as a gift or can we generate our own heat? Where does life and energy come from?

1 J.B.S. Haldane, *Possible Worlds and Other Essays* (London: Chatto and Windus, 1927), 286.

I think it is obvious if we pay any attention at all that the *world* is saturated with energy and light and heat. The world is alive and pregnant, always and everywhere. It sparkles and flames, flows and surges. The problem, when there is one, is in us. What happens to us? Why do we get stuck, knotted, frozen, solidified, inattentive, self-absorbed, idolatrous? How do we get unstuck, untied, thawed out, liquefied, sensitive, sympathetic? These swirling metaphors of fire and water suggest an approach to an answer. I'd like to say that there is a simple answer, but I don't believe that. I think that fear has a lot to do with it, but I am not going to focus on that here. We do need to free the soul from fears, and there are plenty. And there is evil and darkness all around. We all know that. But at the heart of everything is the Imagination and I think that we cannot free the soul from fear or learn to open ourselves to the world in all its glory, complexity and beauty unless we can free ourselves *for* the Imagination. It is the heart, after all, that is the "organ" of the Imagination. And it is in that pulsing, hot and muscular star within us that creation and discovery merge. It is in the heart that the inner and the outer become one. So learning the Imagination is learning the ways of the heart—and this means learning to open to the world. I want us to think about how we can feel more connected to the life of the world, how we can learn to more easily merge with the flame and flow of things. Many of us need a more expansive self. I certainly do. I want to live less trapped inside my head or in an isolated body. We all need the freedom to move around in the world—*all* the world, not just some packaged version of it.

One thing we might do as a start—and this will sound abstract and intellectual, but *it isn't*—is to look for category mistakes. The categories which, mostly unwittingly, provide the framework for our lives serve to mold our experiences and our actions. Our unconscious taxonomies produce the world we know. How we think about people and things, how we speak of them, is not separable from how we experience them, how we feel them, how we interact with them. Our thoughts are not separate from our experience. They do not occur in the head. They are in the world. They are in our bodies. It is not easy to do, but changing your "mind" changes your "world" because your "mind" is more than your mind. Thought, emotion, and sensation all occur together and provide the mood and stance and attitude with which you encounter reality. If you can bring to light your unconscious assumptions about things, you can alter your experience.

The late San Francisco-based poet Leslie Scalapino worked throughout her career to break down the barriers between the inner and the outer, thought and being, mind and experience. Her work is profoundly important for me. Her friend and colleague Lyn Hejinian wrote in her remembrance:

> Leslie's work was a manifestation of what she termed "continual conceptual rebellion." "Continual conceptual rebellion" is a means of outrunning the forces that would re-form (conventionalize) one. If you stay in one place too long you'll be taken over—either by your own fixating ideas or by those of others. To survive one must always be outrunning what she called "the destruction of the world." This is a reason that travel is such an important motif in Scalapino's work.[2]

---

2 Lyn Hejinian, "Leslie Scalapino Remembered," http://www. poets.org/viewmedia.php/prmMID/21547 (accessed 2/16/2015).

Such a conceptual rebellion is a version of what Henry Corbin called "perpetual hermeneutics" and it is a profoundly imaginative process that engages the whole person: body, mind, and soul. My attempts here to engage in a bit of conceptual rebellion are really very conservative – I am not nearly as far along as Scalapino was, and as I think most poets are. But there are probably many ways to effectively rebel, and I am learning. So let's think a bit about a couple categories that I think have trapped me, and probably others as well.

Unmaking a Soul: The Concrete and the Abstract

I want to consider a binary framework that has had a pernicious influence on my life. My sense is that if I free myself from the traps that this frame helps construct, it would go a long way towards making me less cramped, more open, and more graceful moving through my life. There is nothing novel in this strategy – it's a standard poststructuralist move to deconstruct a binary opposition. I've engaged in this sort of thing before, trying to banish simplistic and mis-leading distinctions such as mind and matter, body and soul, myth and history, the inner and the outer. This pair is an integral part of that same complex, but I hadn't been seeing it clearly and it gives us another way of understanding the split psyche of western consciousness. All of these supposedly "objective" and rational distinctions are rooted in our individual psyches in one way or another, and messing about with them can be unsettling and difficult. We are unconscious of so much, and just can't see things that afterwards we think should have been obvious. In my case, the dichotomy in question maps fairly well on to the opposing and, of course, archetypal figures of my father and my mother.

The categories I want to banish are the *concrete* and the *abstract*. Long ago when I was getting my unsettling initiation into the autonomous realities of the psyche I had a bit of an epiphany. It came to me that what was wrong with my life had to do with "abstraction" in some deep sense. I didn't really know what that meant – but I had a strong sense that finding out would be life-changing. I had a clear intuition that I needed to go "down and in" in order to get out of the particular trap I was in. This turned out to be true – and it has taken a very long time to do the deep work necessary – but it is only quite recently that I have begun to really understand the place of "abstraction" in my story. James Hillman gave me the necessary tools, but it took awhile to figure out how to use them.

According to the *Oxford English Dictionary,* the word *concrete* refers to whatever is "available to the senses," "actual, solid," from the Latin *concretus*: "congealed, coagulated, solidified," but it also means: embodied in matter, in practice, or in particular examples. *Abstract* comes from the Latin "to separate or draw away from" and means generally withdrawn, removed or separated from material objects, embodiment, practice or particular instances. Used in this sense it refers to ideas or concepts in contrast to *things*. The distinction is thoroughly modern and dates from the fourteenth century. By the sixteenth century the opposition between the two was fully developed. It presumes and mirrors one of the fundamental dichotomies that characterizes the Western rationalist world view – that between *thought* and *things*. What became the definitive philosophical statement of the metaphysical view of the world that justifies such a distinction we have from Descartes in the contrast between *res extensa* and *res cogitans*. His experience of this schism is most clear in his discovery that the one certain fact he could not *doubt* was *cogito, ergo sum*: I think, therefore I am. The thoughts in the mind are more immediate, more certain than any objects on the outer world. The world of nature is thus separated from us – we have no immediate access to it – it is *present* to us primarily as an *absence* that must be overcome. And this scheme presumes a profound division between our thoughts and our senses. This view of things abstracts us from the world – we need to escape it. It has been argued by many people that this is a development peculiar to Western societies that did not occur elsewhere. There are other options – other ways of conceiving and experiencing both ourselves and the world. We can imagine our way into a different life. If your epistemology has an option besides thinking and sensation then this schism can be overcome. In the story I am telling here, Imagination is that third, essential faculty. The reason for this is that both thought and sensation are subsidiary modes of psychic function, both subsumed within the all-encompassing embrace of Imagination.[3] There are multiple styles and varieties of both thought and sensation, which differ among cultures, within cultures, among individuals, and even within each of us as we make our way through our lives – even, I would argue, through a single day. Our experience is not broken up into "faculties" – the world comes to us whole, complex, living, mysterious, and wild. Our

---

3 Here I depart from Henry Corbin's tripartite cosmology, which he derives from Ibn 'Arabī. Where Corbin emphasizes the intermediate place of Imagination between the categories of the intellect and the modes of physical sensation so that the *mundus imaginalis* is the *barzakh,* I would rather follow another thread in Ibn 'Arabī's thought and see *everything* as a *barzakh.* Then *everything* is ambiguous and intermediate, and all of Creation is ultimately a product of the divine Imagination. This is I think the same fundamental move that James Hillman makes and that differentiates his vision from Corbin's.

response is based on the continuous action and interaction of a continuum of capacities – sensation, perception, fantasy, memory, passions, and intellect – each aspect of which is itself varied, fluid, changeable and unstable.

Both of the categories we're considering, the concrete and the abstract, structure how we respond to the world – there are concretizing and abstracting modes of engagement. Both are useful in their own ways, but since they are elements of our psychic functioning, they have pathologies associated with them that can affect the range and style of our experience in ways that disrupt our lives. What I take to be the legitimate and useful application of this distinction is between the world of particular things and the general ideas we can have of them. Such a division is helpful when we want a simple model of the world so that we can think about and interact with it in some restricted way for some particular purpose. This is how science thinks of the world for the most part. Galileo and Newton provide clear examples of how revolutionary and very fruitful this was in the beginning. Mathematical models of reality have given us modern technology. But the distinction gives rise to a range of troubles if it gets out of hand.

When we lose contact with the Imagination as the central principle of the cosmos, then we lose our experience of the forces in the world that keep everything flowing and alive. When that happens, things tend to get stuck, they stop moving and they die. In the example at hand, a useful, partial and provisional distinction between our mind and things in the world gets reified, frozen, and literalized. Then the archetypal example of something *concrete* is stable, fixed, and absolute – this becomes the measure of the *actual* and real. It is a valuation rather than a description. This makes necessary what we might call a "fundamentalist" attitude towards reality. And on the other side, the *abstract* is divorced from the world of things and is felt to have an independent reality in some disembodied Heaven or realm of Forms in another world. But here, too, the temptation is towards a fundamentalism that posits stability as a prime category of the Real. We are strung between two worlds – unable to *live* in either because both are static and dead. For someone grasped by the concretizing imagination, the *abstract* connotes the useless imprecision and vagueness of the impractical dreamer, the foolishness of an irresponsible escapist. For the lover of the abstracting functions of mind and spirit, the *concrete* denotes the stubborn, fixed, restrictive – all that is heavy and sober and stands in opposition to unfettered freedoms and the glorious chaos of lawless life.

But if we imagine that Imagination lies at the heart of things we can understand the opposition between the concrete and the abstract as a contrast between two different styles of imagining. Then the entire world opens up. Then, when we are standing out in the open, we can feel that there is an underlying pathology that affects both modes of imagining – the concretizing and the abstracting. The pathology is a hypertrophy of the *literalism* that is the hallmark par excellence of the monistic, isolated mind. It's not the "concrete" and the "abstract" that we need to eliminate – it's the *literal* that has to go. The modern meaning for the term, "verbally exact," developed quite late, which should be no surprise, and dates from the sixteenth century. "Literal" derives from the Latin "litera," "belonging to letters or writing." In the fourteenth century it referred to the natural meaning of words and was used as a technical term in biblical exegesis, where four levels of meaning were distinguished: literal, moral, allegorical, and mystical.

Sacred texts were for many centuries understood to be open-ended and overflowing with meaning at every level. A secular, scientific interpretation of a sacred text is left with the literal meaning, and what have come to be called meta-phoric meanings – all originating in the human mind.

So the category of the strictly literal has to go, and with it the intellectual and psychological baggage that it carries. Throw it out. In its contemporary form it is worse than useless; it is stifling. Unchaining those gates grants both things and ideas the spaces into which to flow and blossom, ramify and flame. The literalist vision gives us a world where Things and Mind are independent and medi-ated by language as the bearer of "meanings" connecting the two parts of reality. When we give up the notion of any literal reality we are free to feel the psychic nature of things and the thing-like-ness of thoughts. Mind and nature are not separate. Ideas have body, shape and weight – ideas are alive. And every particular thing we encounter is soaked in feeling, emotion and memory, as well as being open to the gaze of the rational mind. The boundaries are opened. Every *idea* has roots and branches extending beyond our knowl-edge. Every *thing* explodes with life and is in communion with beings all around.

I don't want to resurrect the disjunction between the literal and the metaphoric to describe this situation because it is too loaded with implications I reject. It's true as far as it goes – but it has too many connotations that are tethered to the notion of language as a merely human con-struct. Metaphors are not tropes of poetic thought – they are features of the world. Metaphors exist because the things in the world are intertwined. I would give up the lit-eral/metaphoric pairing in favor of this: the world presents itself as composed of a range of idols and icons. Idols are the literalist knots, the hard parts, the isolated, absolute and imperturbable mirages that are fixed in place by the monistic mind. Icons are all the beings in existence perceived *sub specie aeternitatis*—where each thing exists as and in the infinite, as *saturated*,[4] and ever escaping the bounds of any experience or idea we have—we see icons when the world is dominated by water and fire.

The pathology set things up so that the concrete and the abstract are polar opposites. They are more usefully understood as identical. They collapse into one another and disappear. The literal is always abstract because it posits simplicity and permanence and nothing that exists exhibits either. And the abstract is literal for exactly the same reasons. Both are constructs of a mind seeking universality, unity, stability, and generality. Both are products of a monistic consciousness that does have uses but cannot possibly provide a comprehensive method for understanding the world. If we give up the frame of that world view what are we left with? Without some sort of monism aren't we left in chaos? What we are left with is the *eachness* of things—every thing *is* in an active sense. Things don't just lie there—they *are*! *Being* is an active verb. Each thing *is* itself—each thing individualizes the fragment of creation that it *is*, that it *enacts*. If you want a theological framework for this, then we can say that God manifests throughout Creation as a distributed presence: God is the active source of the unity of beings. God is the Unifier, so everything is particular and wholly saturated—always in excess of any concept or any experience—at the same time. This is what it means to be *concrete*. God is the archetype of the concrete—absolutely individual, fully infinite—the paradoxical

---

4 See chap. 2, n. 47.

unification of the personal and the cosmic, of order and chaos. It is perhaps as a defense against the wild and living power of this divine vision that we have established the barren categories of the literal and the abstract. Eliminate them, and let the wilderness back in.

Being Concrete: A Life in Sympathy with Beings

As a prime example of abstract thinking, the ancient Greek philosopher's distinction between form and matter is at best useful only if taken metaphorically. Charles Olson had it right in 1950 in his essay "Human Universe":

> We have lived long in a generalizing time, at least since 450 BC. And it has had its effect on the best of men, on the best of things. Logos, or discourse, for example, in that time, so worked its abstractions into our concept and use of language that language's other function, speech, seems so in need of restoration that several of us go back to hieroglyphs or ideograms to right the balance.[5]

Ezra Pound was enamored of Chinese ideograms and Olson excited by the Mayan hieroglyphs he saw during his time in the Yucatan. Both thought that such writing must be less abstract, more tied to the world than ours. Ivan Illich saw the development of alphabetic writing as one step in a long process that removed language and meaning from the world and put it inside the heads of human beings. More recently, David Abram and Robert Bringhurst want to put it

---

5 Charles Olson, *Selected Writings* (New York: New Directions, 1950), 53.

back, and they think of reading as akin to tracking and find languages everywhere in the animate world.

Both Form and Matter are abstractions that are hooked in damaging ways to our experience of the world. In themselves they don't probably *cause* any serious pathologies, but they are part of a system of understanding the world that needs to be abandoned if we are to have any chance of living sanely and sustainably on the earth. Form and Matter collapse into emptiness and irrelevance in the presence of *concrete being,* which is where the *life* is. It would be better to imagine ourselves a cosmos that helps us move into that living world. If we try to abandon abstraction and generalization, we are left with the present moment, with particular things. So we have to pay attention. This requires devotion and practice.

It takes practice to attend to people and things in a culture where abstract modes of experience are commonplace. One reason for this is that when abstraction is dominant, feeling tends to be undeveloped. Abstraction is a defensive and isolating stance towards reality. It helps us hold people and things at a distance. It prevents interaction. Recall Jung's scheme of the four functions. Thinking, which is often abstract (but need not be) tends to dominate at the expense of the other rational function, feeling. In a world of abstractions particulars disappear and are replaced by generality and classification: Who am I? I am a white, male, Anglo-Saxon, Protestant New Englander from a middle-class family in the later stages of middle age. I was taken aback recently to find myself pigeon-holed as "crunchy" by one of my younger coworkers. I took umbrage at this, being unfamiliar with this new and dismissive classification for what used to seem a radical and cutting edge lifestyle. So many of the words we use in daily life are really just abstractions, each of which renders invisible vast swaths of experience and indeed obscures most of the wonder and complexity of the world: cold, hot, red, white, black, Latino, gay, straight, love (one four letter word to cover an entire range of human affections and passions!), male, female, democrat, republican, catholic, jew—each of these conjures up an emotional aura lacking precision and particularity, and often indistinguishable from Jung's emotion-laden complex. Feeling on the other hand, is precise and sensitive. It discriminates and evaluates. Simple things escape their bounds. We have to slow way down and our attention is arrested, even to look at simple objects. When feeling is undeveloped, then the world is awash in emotions, which manifest the natural powers of the world undifferentiated by consciousness. Emotions are the un-*felt* energies of things. We don't *feel* them in Jung's sense of the word— we identify with them. Emotion is the result of the influx of forces from outside. It is uncontrolled, indiscriminant, generalized, inchoate, unconscious. Emotions obliterate space and time, and make fine distinctions and perceptions of particularity impossible. Our ability to understand where we stand at any given moment—how our experience is shaped by perception and unconsciousness, feeling or emotion is very much muddied by the fact that emotion and feeling are so closely allied that only rarely, if ever, are they wholly separate. We're always conscious and discriminating as well as unconscious and at sea. It is after all feeling that helps us to discriminate emotions!

Even more deeply damaging, when abstraction dominates and feeling is crippled then a profound disruption of personality occurs. I do not mean merely human subjectivity. We're far outside the subjective-objective divide now. Personification is a fundamental feature of our

experience of the world. You can think of this psychologically as Jung and Hillman do, or you can take a cosmic and
theological viewpoint as Henry Corbin does. In either case
the world is personified – if we are grounded in the reality of
the psyche then we recognize the psychic nature of things
and the partial personalities that inhere in every being. From
the perspective of Corbin and the religions of the prophetic
tradition, all Creation is Personal and each being reflects
the personal nature of the creator. Corbin asks "what would
a world without a Face actually be?" On both of these
accounts the human personality is embedded in a larger
reality that is itself personal but not subjective. Subjectivity
and personality are not two aspects of a single reality, and
personality is not exclusively human. The human person is a
fragment of something larger, and objectively real. Persons
in this sense exist as members of a community – what the
Christian tradition calls a communion. But when abstraction and emotion are in strong tension, the personality of
the world also tends to polarize into Me and the Others. This
me is intensely subjective, possessively self-absorbed, and
set off defensively from the human and nonhuman Others who populate the outside world. Such subjective partial
personalities exist primarily alone – and exist in public space
as members of a crowd, not a community. Both sides of the
division between Me and the Others are drenched in unconsciousness, inarticulate moods and vague generalities. This
is the possessive, personal subject that clings to emotions
and feels that experience is *mine*. This is the version of personhood that most of us identify with. The *ego* exists in this
difficult, emotional realm of the intensive self. Beyond is the
open world of the extensive self where the world and the
human being are both personal but never *mine* – that is the
realm of the community of angels of Corbin's world have

their place and into which we can move as we become conscious enough to escape emotions and begin to *feel*.

You can learn to feel your way into emotions. This
is movement in liminal space – you are *in* them and letting
them have part of you – but paying attention to them as
though you were in some sense outside. In my experience
it is decidedly somatic and kinesthetic. If you are a thinking
type, as I am, this may feel to you like a kind of thought – but
it is tangible thought, occurring in the spaces of your body
and in the world of your surround. It is in this way a form of
alchemy – an operation in and on substances. Some sort of
body work now seems to me essential and it is important
that "somatic studies" are becoming an accepted part of
psychotherapeutic training. Body work is an essential part
of alchemy. One goal of alchemy is to turn a world flooded
with emotion into a diversified landscape differentiated
and amplified by feeling. This occurs by means of operations in matter. Jung's alchemical psychology may seem to
be an intellectualized and spiritualized version of practical,
chemical alchemy, but he was entirely aware that material
grounding was essential and indeed unavoidable. He knew
firsthand that the psychosomatic manifestations of psychopathology are pronounced and often intense. Active
imagination always requires objectification of the imaginal
material as a way of giving substance to the fleeting, elusive
and shadowy visitations from the unconscious. Alchemy is
a mode of "thinking with things" and thinking with your
body and all your senses to explore the topographies of
emotion is without doubt an alchemical operation.

The people and things, the cities and the landscapes, of my world at least, are generally drenched in emotions, though it took me a long time to realize this. This must
be true for others to. An essential part of the mysterious

processes that get lumped together as "individuation" is to distinguish things from yourself, from your body. This is apparently the work of a lifetime: to give the world back to itself. When the ego is born in that first boundary crossing, that primal distinction, it can happen that it retains a strange attachment to things, as if the world belonged to the ego. And so everything is laden with emotions that shift and swell, crash and recede like the tides. If we can keep our heads above water and learn to swim then maybe we can turn these to feelings and find out what there is in the world besides the sovereign ego. This gives the life back to the things from which we have stolen it. This is a kind of pathology of the heart wherein emotions substitute for feeling. In a correlative disorder, the intellect, the thinking faculty, also attempts to engulf the world within itself. Abstract words and concepts, theories and schematic, theory-driven visions all swallow the world the way possessive, complex-driven love swallows the Beloved. The great work then is to come home to yourself and let the world be the world. My suspicion, my intuition, my premonition, and more and more my *experience* is that when you do "find yourself," it will be clear that the tiny spark you tried so hard to protect and defend against the darkness isn't a thing at all. It is the image and symbol of a verb, process, an imperative: Be! It is itself the place where beings, as persons, can come to presence. It is a clearing, an opening, rather than a thing. It is the heart of creation, the Temple where every being shows its Face.

At the Edges of Empire

The temple can be understood as the archetypal "place" where presence occurs—where the world lights up. But the word "temple" may suggest more than I mean to say. For it me it evokes the image of crumbling marble columns on a dry and desolate hill by the sea. That's fine and quite profound, actually—but I want to be careful not to inflate my meaning. This is a temptation for me, and I often succumb to it. I tend to write and think in capital letters: Temple, God, Language, Thought, Idea. Every noun capitalized. That is abstraction again. Let's not do that this time. Not the Temple, but temples—proliferating everywhere. The world lights up in all manner of ways, most of them very subtle, very understated, very small. Maybe even calling these all "templar" occasions is too grandiose, but I do want to suggest connections to traditional religious uses of the term. I just want to make it possible for us to notice even the tiniest glimmers of presence, at every scale.

What unites all these templar events is that they exhibit eachness: they are particular, local, time-bound and unique. They are moments of high-intensity saturation and so are concrete in the sense that I want to mean the word. They stand in opposition to the abstract space and time of modern science, and modern technological life. I have said this in many ways and many times over the years, always trying to get closer to the felt immediacy of these moments of presence. But it was only a few weeks ago that I was really hit by the political meaning of this opposition. Partly this is because our family recently traveled in Ecuador and I've been reading about the history of Latin America and the horrors of colonization and empire have been a lot on my mind. The Mexican poet and essayist Heriberto Yépez has been thinking about Charles Olson and in particular about the very essay "Human Universe" from which I quoted earlier. He points out a profound tension in Olson's essay by showing a thrust in his work that is exactly the opposite of what we were discussing before. Yépez writes,

"There are laws," begins Olson's essay "Human Universe," written in Mexico. How does one create the illusion that there are general laws? The foundation of time reduced to space is, precisely, the supposition that there exist laws that function in the same way (homogeneously) across all (heterogeneous) times. If different times are united by the same laws, then, these times are not separated and thus form a single space... This belief is the basis of totalitarian thought, in all its forms... Imperial ideas transform time into space. Nomadic ideas, on the other hand, tend to understand time as a multiplicity of times. These times – tribes of monads – are autonomous from each other, each one obeying its own laws. (The notion of a single spatialized time is linked to the historical appearance of the State.) The Rarámuri, for example, developed a model based on the existence of more than one internal time, sustaining the existence of various "souls" that simultaneously co-existed within the human body. While the Huichol believe that when a pair of nomad groups meet two different times collide. This understanding of time not only functions to plumb the profound nature of the human animal but also to impede the formation of a unitary political order, a system of centralized control...

> In [Imperial time], time as individual measure, as autochronology, in which each being lives its own chaosmos, is not allowed to exist.[6]

Henry Corbin would have approved. This fits seamlessly into his cosmology – at least as I have understood it. But this vision of autochronologies – multiple, individuated times – does indicate a hinge point we need to think about. This is the difference between what Hillman called a monotheism of consciousness and a full-blown polytheism of consciousness. On the one hand, you have an imperial cosmology with a uniform space and time, with laws that apply everywhere. That uniformity is the God's-eye view of Creation. It is the foundation of every monism. On the other hand, you have a postmodern sort of pluralism with an uncountable number of autochronologies, each being occupying not a unified cosmos along with all the other beings in Creation, but as Yépez says, a "chaosmos." In such a fractured Creation there can be no legitimate Imperial power, no Theory of Everything and certainly no One God. It does seem to me that Corbin tries, I think with success, to have it both ways. He does this by making us understand that the One God is wholly inaccessible, and leaving us with an infinite plurality of Angels – one for every being of Light, he would say. There may be a single unified perspective, a God's-eye view of things, but we certainly will never, ever have access to it, so we may as well stop trying. Our attempts always result in colonization and efforts to establish Empires. This imperial cosmology produces a politics of religion that is always destructive. And the imperialisms

---

6 Heriberto Yépez, *The Empire of Neomemory,* trans. Jen Hofer, Christian Nagler, and Brian Whitener (Oakland and Philadelphia: ChainLinks, 2013).

of science and economics are really little better, as we have learned to our dismay as we watch capitalism and its powerful products disrupt and destroy the local, concrete realities of indigenous societies of resistance everywhere.

But what is the alternative to a grand Theory of Everything, an Imperial, monotheistic vision of the world? Surely we can envision a polytheistic global society–even including a range of monotheisms, Judaism, Christianity, and Islam for example, each claiming to have a partial vision of the truth–such a possibility is presented in the Qur'an in fact. But it is really possible to live with no theory of anything? We always have a frame we see through–a set of categories that structure our experience. What we have to understand is that these are not universal and necessary. There are others–and we might be able to adopt them if we find ours have become stifling and damaging.

In the context of our deconstruction here it is the Imperial categories we need to jettison. The abstract and the concrete as they have been–imperially–understood, have to go. With them goes the correlative notion that meaning inheres in the systematization of knowledge. If you do have an Imperial, law-abiding Universe to live in where everything occupies the same space and endures through the same homogeneous linear time, then it is possible and maybe necessary to understand "meaning" as a characteristic of the system as a whole. "Interpretation" depends upon the fact that things and events in the world are linked together. If you discard all this what we are left with is something like the revelation that Charles Olson had when he read Richard Wilhelm's translation of the Taoist classic *The Secret of the Golden Flower*. There we find a phrase that stunned Olson: "That which exists through itself is what we call meaning."[7] The term Wilhelm translated as "meaning" is *Tao*, but that gets us a bit off the track. For Olson then this led him to conclude "nothing is anything, but itself, measured so."[8] Which is a bit obscure—but the general drift is clear: to know anything is to grasp its uniqueness, and its meaning lies right there. For Olson "each particular becomes meaningful through an act of self-creation."[9] Olson hitched all this to Whitehead's cosmology, which is arguably Imperial at its root—and this is the genesis of the tension in his work that Yépez has pointed to.

In our context this tells us that "meaning" inheres in the *concrete*: whatever exhibits eachness, individuality, precision; and apprehending it requires sensitivity, care, and attention. And the saturation of the phenomenon does lead off in all directions, but mysteriously, and in a manner that defies systematization. The world is infinite but *not* systematic—it cannot be successfully colonized by the Imperial mind. The archetypal locus for this resistance, this saturation, is the temple. The temple is the site where beings *be* themselves, where they are fully present, personal, and substantial.

7 Charles Olson, *Muthologos: Lectures and Interviews,* ed. Ralph Maud (Vancouver: Talonbooks, 2010), 117. See Stephen Fredman, *The Grounding of American Poetry: Charles Olson and the Emersonian Tradition* (Cambridge: Cambridge University Press, 1993), 62ff.

8 Olson, *Muthologos,* 262.

9 Bruce Elder, *The Films of Stan Brakhage in the American Tradition of Ezra Pound, Gertrude Stein, and Charles Olson* (Waterloo, Ontario: Wilfrid Laurier University Press, 1998), 364.

So let's return to the question we began with. My claim is that a temple is anywhere a clearing is, where the spark and the flame are found, where the world is fully alive and present to the imagination. That there are many kinds of temples goes without saying, but I'm not going to attempt a taxonomy here. My question for the moment is simply: What keeps us out? And how do we get in? It will no doubt turn out that it can't be answered simply, but I'm going to make a first attempt. The clearing is what Robert Duncan has called "the place of first permission."[10] I think that often children just *are* there–their imaginations are open to the Imagination of the world–and when the two meet, everything demands attention, everything lights up. This is of course not universally true, but you will all know examples of what I mean. I remember my daughter when she was very young used to delight in worms and snails and insects, which made me happy since I was trained as an invertebrate zoologist. Then she went to first grade and discovered from her female colleagues that all those things are gross and disgusting. It seemed a shame. Part of the world had suddenly gone dark for her. She wasn't interested anymore–her imagination was closed off from that part of reality. This is arguably one small but significant example of what is known among social and political theorists as "cultural hegemony," the process whereby one social group dictates the values and beliefs of another without direct coercion. My daughter had been acculturated into an Empire. You see how easily we fall in line.

Boundaries are established that determine what is worthy of attention, what is important, what can be done,

---

10 "Often I Am Permitted to Return to a Meadow," in Robert Duncan, *The Opening of the Field* (New York: Grove Press, 1960), 7.

said, thought. Hierarchies and systems of thought and behavior organize the universe. Chaos is ordered, individuals are controlled. This happens everywhere there are people in groups – and it happens to isolated individuals living in seclusion. We do it to ourselves if someone else doesn't do it to us. This is partly because we like to belong to groups and we like to feel included – we spontaneously tend to accept the frameworks that others provide us. But it is also because the world seems too huge, too overwhelming, too entirely aweful to bear. We have to restrict our attentions or we fear we will go mad. So in a variety of ways boundaries develop that delimit our world and the range of our actions. It isn't long before we can't imagine anything outside. Truths and habits, assumptions and prejudices become so compelling that we cannot imagine any other life. Many of us really are fearful of letting go of our beliefs, our categories, our schemes for understanding things, for making sense of the world. It must be a rare person – a holy person I think – who can be so free as to cling to nothing at all. It seems to me a worthy goal. That freedom would not be chaos – it would simply be the freedom to respond as appropriately as possible to the circumstances of the moment – influenced by rules and beliefs perhaps, but not bound by them and not frozen into an unthinking automaton.

So how do we prevent such rigidity and freezing of the imagination? How do we keep fluid, supple and alive to the realities surrounding us? We travel. You cannot know your own boundaries until you cross them. This is why Lyn Hejinian points emphatically to travel as an integral part of Leslie Scalapino's attempt to outrun the destruction of the world. Travel doesn't have to be travel in space, though that certainly can have a life-altering effect. You can study history and attempt time travel. You can talk to people who are very different from you. Really talk to them. You can read literature. You can read anything that is outside your comfort zone. You might even make a natural history museum in your room, where every treasure is a mystery, a precious journey away from home. Travel is what gets you into the open. To be in that open place you need to be conscious of where you are, how you are, what frame you occupy. It is a question of recognizing boundaries, which you cannot do unless you move, and can *see and feel* that they are boundaries. Something is on the other side that you do not understand, cannot see, and is a mystery. This applies to every thing there is – every thing has boundaries, needs differentiation from the surround. Everything is in between something and something else and that in betweenness is a boundary. Everything rides that boundary between itself and what is not itself – between itself and something Other – this is the source of the permanent ambiguity of the world. Everything is what it is because of where it is – its boundaries, its place between the clearing and the darkness. As we are always a clearing of consciousness on the edges of unconsciousness. We are always surrounded by darkness all around. This is what keeps us from freezing up. If we forget this, we die. We become idolators of ourselves. This fundamental ambiguity explains the fact that increasingly it seems to me a stunning fact that anyone ever understands anything at all – which *we do!* We sometimes get hold of things for a while. But we forget that our hold is temporary – a kind of gift from the roiling ocean of Being – little islands of stability appear and dissolve at time scales having nothing whatever to do with the lengths of our tiny lives. So many perspectives, so many ways of seeing. I am stunned to silence sometimes by the impossibility of holding anything long enough to speak of it. Anything I say is a partial fragment of something moving at tremendous speed in some other space. This is also why alchemical language in particular, and poetic language in general, is required to make any real sense of the living reality of human existence. I mean you can *do* science and history and make sense of things for a while but it mostly isn't any good at getting at who we are and what we are doing here. Psychological life is far better described by the chaotic, colorful, substantive, messy, and magnificent language of alchemy. There is no attempt at systematic thinking – and anything can turn into anything else in a heartbeat. It is hermeneutics on steroids – it *is* Hermes himself – standing in one autochronology or another – skipping from one to the next and never ever in Eternity as a God's-eye kind of Time of all times – time in cycles, in whirls, in eddies and loops, but not linear history, not Imperial, monotheistic Time. Not ever. Because being concrete means being able to travel in all the times and spaces there are, and being open to the presences of the Others who inhabit them. In the old language we want to discard, they say that this kind of thinking, living, and moving is metaphorical – based on metaphor – and metaphor means "to carry over," which is just what we are trying to do: carry ourselves over the bounds. But there is no metaphor in this new world of the imaginal because metaphor is paired with *literal,* and we now can understand that there is nothing literal – only more or less stable places where beings appear – where they stand out in the light and are present, so that all we can say of them, really, is to speak of them to someone else, someone who we love and have always loved and we say to them just this:

Look! Just look! Look at what there is!

6

Imaginal Love

The Song of the Sensuous

Near the end of *The Dream and the Underworld,* James Hillman writes of the love necessary for working with dreams:

> There is a loving in dreamwork...Let us call it *imaginal love*...This love does not reach only towards unifying as we have been so tediously taught. When we love, we want to explore, to discriminate more and more widely, *to extend the intricacy that intensifies intimacy.*[1]

When I read this amazing book again recently after many years spent thinking about Henry Corbin and the imaginal, I was knocked wide awake by these words, which I had passed over blindly long ago.[2] They seem to me now to express with precision much of what I have struggled to articulate for a long time. We are moved to the heart of what makes Henry Corbin's notion of the *imaginal* so compelling, so mysterious and so fertile. And I am confirmed in my feeling that what Hillman found so powerful in Corbin the man, and in his work, was the display of beauty and a

---

1 James Hillman, *The Dream and the Underworld* (New York: Harper & Row, 1979), 197 (my italics).

2 My thanks to Bill Carpenter and his students at the College of the Atlantic for inviting me to discuss this book, which I otherwise would likely not have revisited.

love for the craft of the imagination that colors all of Hillman's own immense opus. What Hillman focuses on here is
the dreamwork, but the scope of the imaginal far exceeds
those bounds. An imaginal approach to reality provides a
style of consciousness, a metaphor for experience, and a
stance towards reality as a whole.

In this vision of the imaginal, exploration and love
are naturally and necessarily paired. I find it wonderful,
exciting, and, once so clearly stated, quite obvious. "Of
course!" I have to say, how could it be otherwise? Suddenly the world opens up. The primordial order of things is
revealed. We are bound to this world by love and a natural
desire to extend our intimacy with things through exploration. At work here is a trinity of active principles in mutual
and self-reinforcing interdependence: exploring, loving,
and imagining. This provides the outline of an entire cosmology. If we were in a theological mood, we might call
this relation among the principles *perichoresis*, which was
Maximus Confessor's term for the relations of the three
Persons in the Christian Trinity.[3] And indeed for Hillman,
and of course for Corbin, personification and personhood
are fundamental characteristics of reality. And our three
archetypal verbs only have meaning in a cosmos where the
Person is the first and final fact.

We might say that in this trinity, the imagination
corresponds roughly to the function of the Holy Spirit in
Christian theology. Imagining is a "verbal noun" denoting the
mercurial energy that ties everything in Creation together.
In the absence of the activity of imagining, exploration

---

3 *Perichoresis* is derived from the Greek *peri,* "around," and
chorein, which has multiple meanings, among them, "to make
room for," "go forward," and "contain."

fragments into chaotic, destructive curiosity, and love erupts into lust and greed. Without active imagining, the community of our three personified principles breaks apart into a collection of separate and isolated objects. The flame of things flickers out. In the absence of imagination, people wander homeless in an alien world.

Who ever removed us from the wild world? Why do so many feel out of touch with people and things? If we take this cosmology at all seriously, we see that at root this homelessness is the result of a failure of imagination. The cause of this fall, the reason for the loss of soul, ours and that of the world, is a rupture between our individual imaginations and the imaginal ground of being. Imagination, I want to say, can heal that primal wound, that break with the world. Who removed us? Who stifled our imagination? I want to answer, as Corbin did, that there are powers of darkness and constraint against which we have to fight every day. This is the battle against fundamentalism and closure and for the imagination that Corbin waged in all his work. It is true that there are forces ranged against the imagination, but it is not always helpful to go out looking for them, because that directs us away from ourselves. And looking for enemies is not always the most useful thing we can do. I know now that the person I am most able to change is myself. Start there. It may be useful to say not that someone has closed us off from the world, but that we cage ourselves, and continue to do so every day.

So how do we get out of our boxes and back in among the wild energies of creation? *Imagination,* this cosmology suggests. But here I have to be careful. I need to stop and point out a temptation I have long often given in to. It is one of the great virtues of Hillman's work that he tries so hard to teach us to avoid it. It is a kind of linguistic trap that is very easy to fall into. I will show you how it is at work in the story I am telling. There are many reasons for us to hide from the world, but perhaps they are all rooted in fear of one kind or another. One species of fear is the terror of chaos. And one strategy for avoiding chaos is for us to abstract ourselves. "Abstract" in this sense means "to draw away from." An earlier meaning is "abstruse and difficult to understand" and this refers to our *ideas* about things, not to the things themselves. Ideas may indeed be abstruse and hard to grasp, but this is because they are removed from the immediate sensuous realities of the world. This distinction gives rise to the contrast between the abstract and the concrete. But now things get a bit muddled because, for all the difficulties they may present, abstract ideas are in fact far less complex that the concrete realities they purport to describe. Abstraction, in this sense, strives for simplicity, timelessness, universality, and generality. Abstract ideas float somehow in another, less disordered and more elegant world. When we abstract ourselves from this world we escape the concrete, complex particulars and all the messiness and chaos that characterize the living matrix of beings in which everything is embedded. That is why ideas enable us to understand the world: they reduce and simplify it so that the chaos of things can be endured, and often, controlled. Abstraction, in both senses, is a protective strategy. But, and here is the great temptation, we tend to get caught in our abstractions and take them literally, and those simple ideas then become traps and cages. Abstraction generates abstract nouns with abandon.

I have fallen into that trap here already. Let's look at the elements of that Trinity I proposed. I was careful at first to call these imagining, exploring, and loving. But soon enough the abstract nouns start to take over, and we get

"Imagination," "Exploration," and "Love." That sounds important and substantial, indeed "philosophical," as if we have some Fundamental Principles in our grasp. But they are all abstractions. We have to stay with the verbs: imagining, exploring, loving. These are tied to particular acts, and they are inherently plural and pluralizing. We having imaginings, explorings, lovings. All active, all diverse, all ramifying. And as Jung spoke of active imagining, we also have to speak of active exploring, active loving. The more we love and imagine in particulars, the more complex, interesting, manifold and loveable the world is. One could argue, as Corbin does, that just such a problem has long bedeviled Christian theology by making substances, *hypostates,* of the three persons of the Trinity and thus metamorphosing them from active principles into Things. But as Corbin says many times, and many other mystics and theologians have asserted the same over the centuries, God is not a Being, not a Thing. In so far as the persons of the trinity are anything at all, they are not nouns – they are *verbs.* Most of us have that mistake embedded deep within us, and we tend to think of ourselves as things. I mean people are things, aren't they? I mean, there you all sit quite solidly on chairs we quite reasonably call things. Maybe the dominance of a theology of substances in the major monotheisms is part of the reason, or we could go right back to the source in Plato and blame him, as many have done, for seeing the Really Real in the transcendent abstractions that are the Forms. Not every culture shares this view. We might think of the dominance of the verbal form in Hopi, or listen to the Buddhists who have been trying to tell us the Self doesn't exist for two and a half millennia. The person is a verb, not a noun. There is no hard little nubbin of ego anywhere to be found. We are activity all the way down. Try imagining yourself this way.

It's very liberating. And our fundamental actions? They surely include imagining, exploring, and loving.

Wonder and love first draw us out into the world—a passion for things, for beauty, for discovery. We have a natural desire to become intimate with the particular things of the world. As Corbin has taught us, the central faculty of our human *being* is creative imagination, as it is the central driving force of all Creation, and this is how it manifests most powerfully in us: as a drive towards increasing the range and extent of our intimacy—it is a desire to love more widely, more fully, more intricately, more completely. And these intimate movements create a duet, a dance of equal partners, for imagining is both creation and revelation, as any artist well knows. A discovery is always also an invention—to invent is to discover, and comes from the Latin *invenire,* "to come upon." It was only in the sixteenth century, with the appearance of the modern experience of subjectivity, that "invent" came to mean to "make something up," and only then could the imagination lose its rightful place as a feature of the objective world.

It seems to me hardly possible to overstate the importance of imaginal loving for our grasp of what it means to be in the world. Loving is inseparable from exploration, discrimination, and the development of the full range of sensitivities required "to extend the intricacy that intensifies intimacy." This kind of loving is the water of the fountain of life and the essential alchemical fluid that melts the world. It is Hermes/Mercury—messenger of the gods—flowing powerfully through everything there is. Christians have said for centuries that God is Love, and this is a wonderful and very worldly doctrine meant to emphasize our incarnation, our sensuous existence as bodies. But when it goes wrong and God and Love are both treated as substantive and abstract ideals then all Hell breaks loose with a vengeance. God becomes an idol upon whom we project all our fantasies and fears, love loses its anchorage in particular persons and things, and exploration is transformed by the will to power into greed and destruction. Gone is the careful attention to particulars from which we develop both sensitivity and discrimination. All this because, Henry Corbin explains, we lose contact with our Angel, who is the Angel Holy Spirit – the mercurial spirit and the imaginative power in each of us.

As an essential correlate of imaginal loving, this Angel also individuates. Meeting one's angel corresponds to what Jung called individuation. But as Corbin tells us, and Hillman has repeatedly reaffirmed, it is not *my* individuation that is at stake but the individuation of the Angel. Individuation is never "mine" – it has nothing to do with that grasping "me" that always wants, always needs, is always empty and searching for something it will never find. The syzygy with the Angel fills that emptiness, but it does not give you your "Self" – it gives you the world and the imagination for loving in it. Individuation is entry into a personified world, an imaginal world where the person is the first and final fact, but where there are no "egos" – all true love is both egoless *and* personified.

And if loving in this way is required "to extend the intricacy that intensifies intimacy," then it is clear there must be a craft of loving, mirroring that of imagining. Because we are not speaking of "falling in love," or "being in love" that comes on with the "WHAM!" of eros like a force of nature and from the outside. Imaginal love is loving as a verb, which has a specific, particular object, is willed, not compelled, and is in a dance, reciprocally responsive with the object of that love. That reciprocity is made possible by the quicksilver of imagination. A living engagement with the personified world is only possible when the continual action of the imagination provides the matrix in which all sensation and all action occurs. From Corbin's perspective, this fundamental creative imagination is an activity of both the human soul and the soul of the world—it is the divine matrix in which all things *are,* out of which they must arise. In this vision the world is not an object and the lover is not a subject—that disjunctive dichotomy is abandoned. A person exists in an open, imaginal field, a field that is open to and through the world that is itself also personified. Every being *is* as personified and any interaction whatever takes the form of *persons* conjoined by an interpenetrating fluid of silver.

The difficulty of the craft of living and loving in the world is also hard to overstate. This is in part because "the world" can only be glimpsed aslant—we cannot approach it directly. So seemingly evident, so unquestionably, unmistakably *here* as to be beyond question, our experience of the "world" is in fact ambiguous, subtle, shifting, unstable, and mysterious through and through. We miss so much, are unconscious of so much, ignore so much. It is so easy to lose your way. "Being-in-the-world" overwhelms our sensibilities—sight and hearing and touching and tasting—it overwhelms our capacity to feel. But I don't like to use the word "world" because it is so commonplace as to be worse than useless. It suggests, among other things, the world as *known,* by science, by reason, or even by unreason, but in any case it is just a marker for a situation we take for granted—that we are in a world. It's another abstraction. Some of the early phenomenologists tried to get around this and reawaken our sense of wonder by talking about the *Lebenswelt,* the lifeworld, but that is too prosaic. It does nothing to suggest

the really limitless complexity of our situation. And even
"complexity" is a poor and inadequate descriptor – we now
have very sophisticated sciences of complexity – but they
are no help at all in elucidating what I am trying to gesture
towards. We have to bracket the objective, rational sense of
world we mostly assume, and even the everyday life-world
as it is normally lived – that's all there of course, but there is
far more going on, all the time.

Heidegger made some moves in this direction by
emphasizing the pervasiveness and necessity of "moods" –
we are always in a mood, which is experienced as a feature of
our world, not a state of consciousness. But Heidegger, being
interested in metaphysics and ontology rather than psychopathology and depth psychology, didn't take this insight
terribly far. It is useful, at least to begin with, to acknowledge
the ubiquity of what depth psychology has long called "the
unconscious." I think it likely that most everyone knows
that the Unconscious is neither a thing nor a place, and that
it is a very slippery notion indeed. But, when we are being
careless, which for me at least is most of the time, we tend
to speak quite vaguely of both consciousness and unconsciousness and we do feel that both are present all the time.
Most people who are interested in Jung have some real sense
of what living on the liminal edge of unconsciousness feels
like, and that it does tend to make the bottom fall out of
everyday life – and so it has the salutary effect of opening
up the world. Often in startling and uncomfortable ways,
to put it mildly. But that's still not enough ambiguity to get
us where I want to go. This abstract opposition still tends to
place consciousness in us, in opposition to the world, and in
opposition to unconsciousness, which is pretty clearly not in
us, but does often tend to feel oppositional. The point I want
to make is that the dichotomy between consciousness

and unconsciousness, wherever we try to locate them, is unhelpful and limiting. To generate some sense of the infinite intricacy and subtlety of the "lifeworld" we have to come to feel that the concept of "consciousness" masks just as much reality as does the word "world."

What we have come to call "the objective world" is astonishingly deep, rich, intricate, ambiguous, and ramifying beyond our abilities to imagine—"the world is stranger than we *can* suppose"—but so also is the other pole of that dichotomy we need to abandon, the subject. People speak rather glibly of consciousness and of the unconscious, as if the one could be represented by a large well-lit room that we all stand in together, the "global community," and the other by some uncanny dark place, lights off, monsters lurking, an abyss into which we fear to fall. And notice: many of us who habitually speak of "consciousness" will by contrast say "the unconscious"—nobody ever says "the unconsciousness." This language habit suggests that the unconscious is a place, although we have no idea where it is, whereas consciousness is simply an openness to the world, which is after all *right there.* At the same time, many of us think of consciousness as the prime location of what makes each of us individual, uniquely the person who we think we are. Consciousness is openness to the world, but each of us is looking out of our own window, and for most of us in this crazy technical culture, consciousness is somehow located in the room we stand in, somehow "in our heads." None of this makes a whole lot of sense. Where is consciousness? Where is unconsciousness? Where is the world? Where is the "me" who I am? Where are you? How are they all related? Consciousness, the unconscious, me, you, the world—what is all this? We sort of have the sense, many of us I think, that these are all interrelated and interpenetrate

somehow, but it is very unclear how. This supposedly com-
monsense construction doesn't make any sense. The trouble is that these words we use to structure experience are
all abstract nouns. None of them really have any referents.
We are far better off giving them up and speaking about
what is happening – by using verbs and adverbs and speaking of events rather than objects. This is very hard to do
because our habits are so ingrained and English in particular
is so loaded with abstractions. Arabic, we are assured, is far
better, as is Hopi, apparently. In some other life I would very
much like to be a linguist so I could know this firsthand. But
if you are as effectively monolingual as I am, then at least
you can read, write, and maybe even speak poetry. Or at
least drama. Be dramatic – it will get you much further than
being analytic. Literature of all kinds tries to save us from
abstraction and get us to particulars, to narrative, to feeling.
James Hillman has long argued persuasively that the language of psychology is hopelessly inadequate to the task of
describing, let alone explaining, psyche and human life, and
that it is in myth and literature that we will find the models
we need to understand ourselves.

If we pull those little boxes off and toss them away –
consciousness, the unconscious, the world, me, you – then
everything bursts into life, with an energy and a fecundity
far beyond our abilities to imagine. We are like Darwin or
Wallace or von Humboldt standing amazed on the edge
of a New World. And maybe we have a chance, like most
boxed-in nineteenth-century Europeans did not, to be
explorers and discoverers who are simultaneously lovers
and creators rather than conquerors and destroyers. But
with those boxes gone it is clear that this rich, mysterious
new world ranges beyond what we have caged in as the
"outer" world, but encompasses, too, everything we have

put in the box marked "inner." We say "consciousness" so easily, so unconsciously, as if we knew what we are talking about, as if it were simple. Now we know it is not an abstract thing of any sort, but more like an activity. But that isn't nearly enough–we need to open it up wider than that. The activities and styles of awareness are multiple, varied, elusive, ambiguous, and our terms to describe and discover them need to be unlimited by preconceptions. There are limitless varieties of awareness. Hillman has done a great service by resurrecting the pantheon of ancient Greek gods and goddesses to help us find mythic resonances for some of these styles of knowing, sensing, being, and doing. Without some such vocabulary we are hopelessly opaque to ourselves, and the primary potential of human experience is impoverished and depauperate. We can turn to literature and poetry for a kind of natural history of consciousness, for compendia, bestiaries, herbaria, zoos, gardens, all open for us to walk in and live in, to *use* as aids to metamorphosis. Corbin called for a perpetual hermeneutics of the Word. The poet Leslie Scalapino, in a striking postmodern echo, has called for a perpetual conceptual rebellion. Both recognized that we need a perpetual revolution in language. Both were aware that we are verbs and that life exists only as movement, a perpetually unstable equilibrium between order and chaos.

Let's pull Heidegger into this again. His analysis of what he called our being-in-the-world emphasizes the prime importance of moods, as I've mentioned. We all know there are lots of moods and that they can dominate our experience. But there is something quite wonderful that is lost to those of us who know Heidegger only in translation. In German, the word for mood is *Stimmung*. According to the composer Karlheinz Stockhausen, who wrote a choral work of that name, the word means "tuning," but it really should be translated with many other words because *Stimmung* incorporates the meanings of the tuning of a piano, the tuning of the voice, the tuning of a group of people, the tuning of the soul. This is all in the German word. Also, when you say: We're in a good *Stimmung*, you mean a good psychological tuning, being well tuned together.[4]

This is just marvelous for us because of the central place of music in Henry Corbin's account of the imagination. The notion of harmony and harmonic resonances among the different worlds in the imaginal realm is a central metaphor in all his work. He draws on Platonic and Neoplatonic notions of harmony and the music of the spheres, which have had such an important role in the theologies of the monotheistic religions and among mystics in every tradition. I would like sometime to see Corbin's copy of *Being and Time*—I would be surprised if the sections on *Stimmung* did not have some most revealing annotations. He was deeply immersed in Islamic mysticism at the time and many of his notes to the text are in Arabic. I have no doubt he read *Stimmung* as a kind of harmonics, and a proper analysis of moods as a variety of cosmological music theory. Imagine how it might change psychotherapy if it were treated as a form of musical composition or improvisation. That gives another layer of meaning to Jung's dedication to the amplification of images. We could turn up the sound.

We need to have available a wide-ranging, rich, and suggestive vocabulary to talk about and help deepen and intensify the various kinds of consciousness that we

---

4 Jonathan Cott, *Stockhausen: Conversations with the Composer* (New York: Simon and Schuster, 1973), 162.

have, and to make even more available to us. Imaginal loving requires styles appropriate to exploration, attention, and articulating experience so as to expand the range of our intimacy. We want perhaps not "complex" psychology in which the complex is seen as pathology, but a complex psychology where each complex is recognized as a constellation of distinct but related styles of imagining, and the pathology lies in getting stuck in only one. That was Hillman's vision.

Corbin liked to speak of *psycho-cosmology* as a unified world view and saw no chasm between psyche and world. It was all Creation for him, all part of the imagination of God and all of it tied together by sympathy, nostalgia, harmony and the energies of love. That style of imagining seems to me to provide us with an orientation that can help cure any tendencies towards abstraction and compartmentalization and help to free us for the intimacies that the world demands. One strategy is to imagine the simple, abstract words that we favor – love, imagination, person – in ways that extend the range of their reference and make them useful for life. Don't let them hang there, hovering above your head in some postmodern analog of Plato's disembodied, transcendent realm – in, as we say, The Cloud. Let's take them all downward, into the gritty, messy, confusing sensuous world. Let's imagine that it makes sense to say that your fingertip can love the surface that it touches and that the surface loves it by touching back. Let's take these terms that have come to mean something general and vague and abstract and extend them out and down and in so that they are *active* and full of the energy that carries a transcendent reference down into the most minute particular. That is what Corbin would mean by *theosophia*: a transcending wisdom that penetrates into all things. For this theology, to be incarnate means that all our perception can be a kind of loving.

A Marriage of Heaven and Hell

James Hillman was a harsh critic of "spirituality" and spiritual disciplines, but he revered Henry Corbin and his work and was perhaps his most important creative interpreter. He thought of Jung and Corbin as founding figures of equal rank for his own "archetypal psychology." For many years I have been reading Corbin and Hillman side by side and interpreting each in terms of the other. In spite of striking and radical differences between them, I think that Hillman gives us some of the most effective concepts and vocabularies with which to enact and embody many aspects of Corbin's great cosmology of the imagination, which refuses any chasm between psyche and world—it is, he says, a psycho-cosmology. For instance, in *Dream and the Underworld,* Hillman details the kind of attention needed to enact imaginal loving at the immediate level of everyday sensation. He describes the effect of the "underground perspective" that is necessary for dreamwork, but immediately transfers it into the context of the dayworld. We are to use a dreamwork approach to our imagination and experience of the dayworld. That is, we are to be attentive to ambiguity, metaphor, polysemy and mystery—our approach to knowing everything is to be founded upon an essential unknowing. We are to live with one foot firmly planted in each world. Corbin would say we have to see both the Dark Face and the Light Face of things simultaneously. Then, from this "underground" perspective

> the place of one's sensitivity may move from eye
> to ear, and then through the senses of touch, taste

and scent, so that we begin to perceive more and more in particulars, less and less in overviews. We become more and more aware of an animal discrimination going on below our reflections and guiding them... Once we *deliteralize sensation* and take our senses too as metaphorical modes of perceiving, we are finally across the bridge and can look back on the all-too-solid brick structure where we live our lives as man-made defenses against the soul, as an "anthropomorphism called reality."[5]

It took me many years to get a real feeling for the operation of deliteralization. It is archetypal psychology's way of "letting go:" dropping down into the underworld, freeing yourself up for exploration and love, escaping the manifold trappings and traps of fundamentalism, relaxing into the mystery that envelopes us. The work often begins with dreams, because they are clearly not literal reality, but images of it. So sometimes Jung and Hillman will say that we must take them literally. But it is better to run it the other way and say that the dreams stay the same and everything else gets treated *like* a dream. Or you can go right to literature and make the move there, since literature is *fiction* by definition, and not literal. It is the stories we tell ourselves that make our lives miserable, but also it is through stories that we are healed. And this metaphoric and poetic approach to reality is also the foundation for the efficacy and power of an alchemical approach to psychotherapy. Alchemy *cannot* be taken literally and yet it provides a profound world of metaphors for the life of the psyche.

---

5 Hillman, *Dream and the Underworld,* 192-93 (my italics). The quoted phrase is from *C.G. Jung Letters,* vol. 1: 1906-1950, ed. G. Adler and A. Jaffé; trans. R.F.C. Hull (Princeton, N.J.: Princeton University Press, 1973), 214.

Undercutting our sense the literal reality of things is not particularly easy. Our resistance to it is intimately and inextricably tied to that most radically intractable Complex that wants and needs to take things literally, that holds on tight to the world and wants to make everything solid, and ultimately *mine*: the Ego. Of course that's another abstraction, and there isn't "an ego" – but there are psychic energies that seem to constellate together. In most definitions of ego these are mostly functions of control and regulation, which when they are overdeveloped are just what is required to make traps and cages. And of course, "reality testing" is one of those functions and what Jung discovered is that the first thing you have to give up, or at least loosen considerably, in order to do active imagination at all, is that rational Judge who sits on his high bench and tells us what is real and what is "just in our imagination." He has to be disbarred.

Ego functions, within limits, are necessary and admirable. It's only when they hypertrophy that trouble arises. But one particularly intricate and difficult set of problems comes about, on Hillman's account, when anima functions get mixed in with ego functions. I speak of this with trepidation because I am particularly unconscious about anima. She is after all the figure that mediates unconsciousness so that is no surprise, but some of us are more tangled up with her than others. In any case here is a story that I find helpful. One of the many effects of anima consciousness is that she makes us feel the "personality" of the personified cosmos we inhabit. She awakens both the *anima humana*, and the *anima mundi*: the human soul and the soul of the world. Without her there can be no faces, and as Corbin says, "what would a world without a look, without a Face, without a *look*, actually be?" Kant left out the most important category when he laid out his transcendental conditions for the possibility of experience. He recognized space and time, but left out personhood, "personality," as an essential part of "God's sensorium" – which is what Newton called space, wanting to ground it in the Absolute. So anima is essential for experience, but she also causes no end of troubles. When this general sense of personality gets too dominant, then my personality hypertrophies, and everything revolves around me. I become needy and grasping and want the cosmos to be mine. Experiences are blown out of proportion and become *mine* alone. My love is the greatest, my pain is the worst, my joy the most powerful, my anguish the deepest, my life the most significant – all of it special, unique, enormously important, blotting out everything and everyone else. This, of course, is a completely unsustainable level of intensity and self-absorption, and so it collapses into despair and depression. Which are, of course, the worst despair and depression, because they are only *mine*. All this soaking in emotion, taking everything so personally, completely unbalances our relations with the multitude of other persons in the world, and blinds us to the subtle kinds of personification that fill the cosmos. There is no chance whatever for discriminating attention, or feeling with precision. We live in a bubble, lost to the world.

The really profound point is that we can distinguish between "personality," the personal nature of the cosmos, and that pathological version of it that inheres in individuals when the ego gets tangled that way with anima. It's that pathology that is generally meant when people speak disparagingly of the ego and argue that we should be rid of it. Memory and a sense of continuity and all the other ego functions are pretty nice to have. It's this other messiness that causes so much trouble. And here again the Buddhists have been very good for a very long time at telling people to just let go of all that ego nonsense – that it doesn't, you and I don't, exist – or do so only tenuously as a bundle of activities. But if that is true, then what about the personification that is the ground of all experience, of everything that is? There is an "impersonal" kind of personhood. True personhood, the kind we might aspire to, is egoless and strangely "impersonal," free of the grasping neediness that makes us possessive, gives us that desire to make things *mine*. It is I think very much the goal of individuation as Jung thought of it, and certainly as Corbin thought of it. Hillman is suspicious of individuation entirely because he thinks it smacks of salvation, which he thinks isn't possible, but that is another story. Buddha certainly thought that salvation, nirvana, was something like this freedom from attachment based on that needy *me* that arises when anima and ego tangle that way. So let's not be too hard on ego functioning – it's useful. But be ever wary of that demonic possession by possessiveness that makes me feel that I am uniquely *me*. Jung has said more than once that it is when we feel most intensely *unique* that we are most like everyone else. We are truly unique, truly individual, when we are free, when we have forgotten ourselves and are open to the flow of things.

This basic account suggests that the components in the psychic work of a human life are threefold: the encounter with the shadow, which Jung called the apprentice piece, the struggle with anima, which he thought of as the masterpiece, and both of these are in the service of the ultimate goal of letting go of the grasping ego. That possessive and self-absorbed ego, cut off from the freely flowing energies of Creation, is what the Sufis call *an-nafs al-'ammārah,* the lower soul. Achieving that ultimate selflessness seems to me to be a goal worth pursuing, though it seems to me nearly unattainable. I don't think these "stages" are sequential, but it seems useful now to distinguish these three moments in the long work, the opus, which is the alchemical, psychic drama. Unlike Hillman, I think there is value in some notion of salvation, but at the same time I share his deep suspicion of any spiritual path that might make us hope to escape the conditions of this incarnate existence. Salvation it seems to me is best understood, not as an escape from the world but rather as an intensification, an increase in our loving, our care, concern, and compassion that results from an increase in the depth and degree of our incarnation. Such an intensification of the animate, personified world is only possible to the degree that the individual, pathological "person" is diminished. When I shrink, the world expands.

This intensification of life, of the animate, is what Hillman calls "soul-making." He adopts John Keats's notion that "the world is the vale of soul-making." This work is a difficult, imaginative activity that requires care, attention, effort, and skill. It is a craft that can be, must be, learned slowly, over the entire span of one's life. There is no end to learning the ways of the soul. Soul-making is the supreme discipline. Taking up its challenge means there can be no closed regions in all the cosmos from the first circle of hell to the highest rank of the angels. To inhabit a world that vast, the pathological "I" has to shrink to vanishing. Understanding what soul-making really means, grasping the implications for your life, requires the largest possible context. All doors must be open. A sufficiently deep and rich understanding of what Creation *is* leaves no choice—we are called to soul-making by our very nature. Soul-making and psycho-cosmology are necessary complements. Each implies, and requires the other. If you understand the range and scope of psycho-cosmology, then you are immediately called to soul-making. If you feel the depth, challenge, and beauty of soul-making, then you must have world enough to exercise it – the only world adequate is opened to us by the notion of psycho-cosmology. If we accept the derivation of the world *religion* from the Latin *ligare*, to bind or connect, then this necessary connection between the essential activity of the soul and the fabric of the cosmos itself is religious in the deepest sense. This is the lesson of Heraclitus's fragment B45: "Traveling on every path you will not find the boundaries of the soul, so deep is its measure." The quest is infinite. It fills all creation. And so we return to the three interwoven components of imaginal love: exploring, loving, and imagining. And now we can see that soul-making is the supreme exploration – it is the cosmic Quest. But cosmic in an intimate sense – as God says in the Qur'an, He is closer to you than your jugular vein. Everything in your life is an opportunity for soul-making. Nothing falls outside. I think of a quip by Garrison Keillor: "Nothing bad ever happens to a writer – it's all *material*." Same for soul-making.

But there a subtle caution. The infinite cosmology necessary is infinite in the sense of boundless, of not having regions marked No Trespassing. It is not necessarily infinite in mere size, though it could be that too. When I was young I was a passionate reader of science fiction, and an easy mark for the romance of the notion that humanity is destined to colonize the universe. Though I must say that Ray Bradbury's dark realism gave me a certain scepticism even then. Now of course, after *2001: A Space Odyssey, Stars Wars, Star Trek,* and a multitude of spin-offs from these grand epics of deep space, there are few people in the so-called developed world who have not got this notion into their heads, whether they take it very seriously or not. But from the point of view of soul-making, that quest to expand our the species into the galaxy seems small-minded and claustrophobic. The universe as conceived by modern science isn't nearly big enough. And this extraterrestrial quest is an escapism of the sort that is incompatible with soul-making. For soul work, though it surely must include the flights of fancy that give rise to fantasies of escape, is predominantly immediate, incarnate, embodied, rich, sensuous, and grounded.

On Hillman's account, one of the chief characteristics of human life is pathology. Pathologizing is in fact one of the main activities of the soul. In practice I see no reason to doubt this in my own life. It might seem that the main question about pathology, especially psychopathology, is whether we can expect to ever escape it. Hillman thought not; Corbin thought yes, of course; Jung I am not so sure about. But I think asking that question deflects us from something more immediate and perhaps more important. And there Hillman and Jung are brilliant. For the task of soul-making depends upon pathology and what we learn from it—the value that it has in our daily lives. And this is the thing that many therapies miss. We all want escape from our various madnesses and self-destructions, but the hard thing to learn is that the only real way to escape is to acknowledge and suffer through them—again and again—until we discover those aspects of ourselves and the world our maladies are trying to show us. Jung said that in the modern world the gods have become diseases, and Hillman worked for years on that theme. Here he is on the craft of soul work:

> Soul-making is like any other imaginative activity. It requires crafting, just as do politics, agriculture, the arts, love relations, war, or the winning of any natural resource. What is given won't get us through; something must be made of it. There

> is evidently in the soul something that wrests it
> out of the only natural: we experience this twist
> as perversion or the torment and torture of
> pathologizing and are then forced to grope our
> way through the twisted and tortuous labyrinth
> of soul-making. Analysis is the scrutiny of these
> twists and turns in our nature, which we call com-
> plexes, and it aims towards a *lysis,* a way out.[6]

But the analysis called for takes a form in keeping with the act of imaginal loving: it is detailed, exploratory, and cre- ative. And it is based on images. A dream, or a dayworld fan- tasy is never explained away, reduced to the effect of some external cause, but it is expanded, examined, explored, revealed. This analysis is sensuous, incarnate, and devoted to the full reality of all these images of psyche. So much of the rationalist approach to pathologies of all sorts is a technologically sophisticated version of Scrooge's immedi- ate response to the vision of Marley's ghost in *A Christmas Carol,* which he explains away with annoyance and scorn. "Why do you doubt your senses?" Says Marley. "Because," said Scrooge, "a little thing affects them. A slight disorder of the stomach makes them cheats. You may be an undigested bit of beef, a blot of mustard, a crumb of cheese, a fragment of an underdone potato. There's more of gravy than of grave about you, whatever you are!" It's the same thing when we take Prozac and deny the meaning of depression and the strange and terrible moods and disruptions it engenders. We want a physical cause for our problems – so we can take a pill or put an electrode in our brains – this is the underdone potato theory of psychopathology. The soul demands and deserves more.

---

6 Ibid., 129.

Hillman writes, "Analysis of course means making separations and differentiations. A dream is pulled apart, even violated, and this is indeed the necessary destructive work of intellect and of discriminating feeling…" But crucially, "analytical tearing apart is one thing, and conceptual interpretation another. We can have analysis without interpretation. Interpretation turns the dream into its meaning. Dream is replaced with translation."[7] So clearly physical causality is not appealed to and the underdone potato strategy is completely abandoned, but so too is *any* theory of causation beyond what is found in the images themselves. No Freudian symbolism, not even Jungian symbolism. Just the images. A snake is not a phallus in disguise. A witch is not the negative anima. We ask of the images instead: Where to they lead? What do they suggest? How do they look? Smell? Feel? Taste? Who after all are they? Who is appearing to me? What do they want? How can I best respond to this personified world that is opening to me? Analysis cannot reduce—it has to amplify, expand, open, lead onward.

Now we arrive at the climax of the story, because we need to make explicit Hillman's creative interpretation, his "misreading," of Corbin's most central notion, *ta'wīl*. It is spiritual exegesis, spiritual hermeneutics, by means of which we come to understand the meaning of symbols, whether they appear in dreams, in a sacred book, or in the grand text of Creation. Corbin adopts the idea from the Ismaili Shi'ites. He says it is the central principle in all spiritual disciplines. Listen closely because this is quintessentially Corbin: The *ta'wīl* is "the mainspring of every spirituality, in the measure to which it furnishes the means of

---

7   Ibid., 130.

going beyond all conformisms, all servitudes to the letter, all opinions ready-made... [It is] a procedure that engages the entire soul because it brings into play the soul's most secret sources of energy."[8] In *Dream and the Underworld*, Hillman quotes from the third volume of Corbin's *En Islam iranien* on Shiism and Sufism, where we are told that the literal meaning of the Arabic term is to "bring something back," in the sense of "take something home" to its origin and principle. In that chapter Corbin is giving an account of the seven esoteric senses of the Qur'an and is explaining the writings of a nineteenth-century Iranian imam, Ja'far Kashfi. He continues, "*ta'wīl* is the name that one gives in general to all symbolic exegesis... It is a science which has as its pivot a spiritual direction and a divine assistance. When the intention, the capacity and the [divine] aid are united and the end is attained, happiness is complete."[9] Corbin's context and intent are wholly spiritual, mystical, and esoteric. Hillman's appropriation is in so many ways radically different, particularly in *Dream and the Underworld* where the downward pull of death, Pluto, and Hades is often overwhelming, to the point where a friend of mine gave up trying to teach it to undergraduates because they found it too dark and depressing. And Corbin was evidently himself unhappy in the extreme with the uses to which Hillman and some of his colleagues had put the notions of *ta'wīl* and the imaginal. Yet I have to say that Corbin's life-work of bringing these Persian and Islamic theologies to life and light was surely bound to result in their uses in new

---

8 Corbin, *Avicenna and the Visionary Recital,* 28 (see chap. 3, n. 22).

9 Henry Corbin, *En Islam iranien: aspects spirituels et philos-ophiques III: Les fidèles d'amour–Shî'isme et soufisme* (Paris: Gallimard, 1973), 215.

and creative contexts. Many have argued that Corbin himself did much the same and misinterpreted his sources in accordance with his own spiritual project. And in the end I find Hillman's creative hermeneutic of Corbin's work to be rich, fertile, brilliant, and wonderful. Corbin at his best was always the champion of the heretic, the creative genius, the spiritual master who would not be bound by the constraints of institutionalized religion of any sort. Listen to him again as he defines *ta'wīl* as "the mainspring of every spirituality...that engages the entire soul because it brings into play the soul's most secret sources of energy." This seems to me to be a license to love, to imagine and to explore if ever there was one. Hillman tells us that *Dream and the Underworld* is

> an essay in *epistrophē,* reversion, return, the recall of phenomena to their imaginal background. This principle–regarding phenomena in terms of their likenesses–derives more immediately from the work of Henry Corbin, a friend at Eranos, and the method of *ta'wīl* that he has so profoundly explained and illustrated in his own immense work.[10]

In a note he quotes from Corbin's *Creative Imagination in the Sufism of Ibn 'Arabī*:

> In *ta'wīl* one must carry sensible forms back to imaginative forms and then rise to still higher meanings; to proceed in the opposite direction (to carry imaginative forms to the sensible forms in

---

10 Hillman, *Dream and the Underworld,* 4.

which they originate) is to destroy the virtualities of the imagination.[11]

The motion of *ta'wīl* for Corbin and his spiritual masters is vertical. That upward-tending energy is a constant theme in Corbin's work. It is absent almost entirely from Hillman. He wants to carry the sensible back to the imaginative, but refuses adamantly to float upward while doing it. He does, however, very much want the ontological grounding that Corbin's cosmology provides. The imaginal background towards which *ta'wīl* moves us is for Corbin an objective, real world, accessible only to the imagination—this is the *mundus imaginalis,* the inter-world mediating between spirit and sensation. I quote Hillman at some length:

> From Corbin…comes the idea that the *mundus archetypalis*…is the *mundus imaginalis*… [It] offers an ontological mode of locating the archetypes of the psyche, as the fundamental structures of the imagination or as fundamentally imaginative phenomena that are transcendent to the world of sense in their *value* if not their appearance. Their value lies in their theophanic nature and in their virtuality or potentiality, which is always more than actuality and its limits… The *mundus imaginalis* provides for archetypes a valuative and cosmic grounding, when this is needed, different from such bases as biological instinct, eternal forms, numbers, linguistic and social transmission, bio-chemical reactions, and genetic coding.[12]

---

11 Ibid., 203n1 (*Creative Imagination,* 240 [see chap. 3, n. 7]).

12 James Hillman, "Sources of Archetypal Psychology" in *Archetypal Psychology,* Uniform Edition of the Writings of James Hillman, vol. 1 (Putnam, Conn.: Spring Publications, 2013), 15.

Notice particularly how he sees the *mundus imaginalis* as different from a world of eternal forms, the latter being that world of spirit that he so much wants to expunge. But I am not at all sure that he can avoid Corbin's thorough-going spirituality so easily. Corbin would argue that if you disconnect the imaginal world from the worlds that it mediates, it loses its meaning and its reality. It is the higher spiritual world that grants ontological reality to all the lower worlds. Corbin's tripartite cosmology cannot be analyzed into its component parts without destroying it.

But certainly as important for Corbin as the movement to spirit is the refusal to destroy the virtualities of the imagination, and that is why Hillman really latches onto Corbin's project. The move to the imaginal is towards multiplicity and freedom. Hillman sees the spiritual direction as unnecessary and, in fact, generally harmful. He is far more securely attached to the sensible world than Corbin, who was extremely sensitive to the pull of other worlds. Corbin's student, friend, and colleague Daryush Shayegan tells the following story:

> I remember a trip we took together to Isphahan. We were settled in a little lunchroom of the Hotel Shah-Abbas, which reproduced, after a fashion, the small empty niches of the music room of the Palace of Ali Ghapou. In the walls and the partitions there were cut out of the emptiness innumerable small silhouettes of vases, flasks, laces of cuttings of all the forms conceived by an overflowing imagination. It gave to the space a sensation of levitation, the feeling that everything was in suspension. Everything seemed to be an apparition, vanishing as in a dream. I saw Corbin rise, his eyes lit by

an interior gaze, then he took me by the arm, and led me to one of these empty niches, said to me in a voice soft and sensual, "This is the phenomenon of the mirror, put your hand into this space and you will touch no form there; the form is not there: it is elsewhere, elsewhere..."[13]

For Hillman it is the return, the reversion to archetypes and the "virtualities" they represent, that is important, and not the direction:

Reversion through likeness, *resemblance,* is a primary principle for the archetypal approach to all psychic events. Reversion is a bridge too, a method which connects an event to its image, a psychic process to its myth, a suffering of the soul to the imaginal mystery expressed therein. *Epistrophē,* or the return through likeness, offers...a main avenue for recovering order from the confusion of psychic phenomena... [I]t makes us look again at the phenomenon...to find which of many archetypal constellations it might resemble. *Epistrophē* implies return to multiple possibilities, correspondences with images that cannot be encompassed within any systematic account.[14]

Epistrophē is a term from the allegory of the cave in Plato's *Republic.* There it signifies both the enlightenment conversion and the subsequent return of a man freed from the realm of the illusion and shadow who has seen the truth and light of the sun. The traditions that Hillman and Corbin

---

13 Daryush Shayegan, "Le Sens du *Ta'wīl,*" in *Henry Corbin,* ed. Christian Jambet (Paris: Cahier de l'Herne, 1981).

14 Hillman, *Dream and the Underworld,* 4.

both claim, each in a more or less idiosyncratic way, are, broadly speaking, Platonic and Neoplatonic. Corbin represents certain aspects of the Christian and Islamic mystical traditions, both of which are intimately tied to aspects of Platonism, and Hillman, ever the pagan, bases much of his work directly on Greek thought from the pre-Socratics on, and on Renaissance humanism, which attempted to resurrect an ideal of the Platonic academy. The very notion of archetype derives ultimately from Plato's theory of Forms, though in Jung the archetype is much more like a Kantian category than a Platonic Form. For Hillman, as for Jung, the archetypes have only a passing relation to Platonic Forms–they provide the fundamental structures of the psyche and the motifs and figures of myth. Reversion to an archetype is not a move toward abstraction or spirit but to an overflowing source. Dream images are not pale copies of the truly real Images they reflect as they are in a vision shaped by Platonism. Jung and Hillman approach archetypes with no expectation of underlying Unity. Corbin, monotheist, must. A history of the nearly limitless metamorphoses of "Platonic" thought would have to include, at least, an account of all Western philosophy and of all the theologies of the great monotheisms. But however it came about, and however distant from Plato's original intent, for both Hillman and Corbin, the archetypes act as nodes of energy from which the endless varieties and glories of the world emanate and towards which we may return in search of the fountain of creativity from which all life derives.

Hillman is quite explicit about this. He writes that *ta'wīl* "gives a sense of primordiality, of beginning at the beginning; it gives, in Bachelard's words, "a mad surge of life."[15] Gaston Bachelard, the great philosopher of the imagination, wrote: "As I see them the archetypes are reserves of enthusiasm that help us believe in the world, to love the world, to create our world."[16] This is Hillman's vision too, and the return of images to their imaginal ground is never an escape, it is for the love of the world. This is even clearer when Hillman takes another cue from Corbin and affirms that ta'wīl is an exit from the world. But where the gnostic in Corbin experiences that exit as salvation and an escape from the "cosmic crypt," for Hillman, it is temporary – rather like taking a deep breath, seeking the primordial energy at the source. "We move from a dream to this joyfulness in the world not directly, dream to world, but indirectly, dream to archetype to world, and the first step, ta'wīl, is an exitus from the world."[17] In order, we can say, to love it better, to love it more.

And the direction of that exitus? Down, of course. The dreamwork leads us away from life; it leads down and in. We have already heard that dream analysis is "the necessary destructive work of intellect and of discriminating feeling." And we know that this analysis is not interpretation but rather amplification and exploration. But he also has this to say:

> We might call [analysis] the Western version of ta'wīl. It is an effort of intelligence that leads us into the dream, the effort of following its imaginatively deformative leads, where exegesis is exitus,

---

15 Ibid., 132.

16 *On Poetic Imagination and Reverie: Selections from the Works of Gaston Bachelard,* trans. and ed. Colette Gaudin (Putnam, Conn.: Spring Publications, 2014), 151.

17 Hillman, *Dream and the Underworld,* 132.

> leading life out of life, where dream interpretation
> is not a life science but a death science, like phi-
> losophizing which too was once considered to be
> a leading of life towards death.[18]

Corbin's exitus is spiritual salvation; this is something quite different. Where Corbin is oriented unceasingly towards the Light, Hillman's instincts drive him down towards the darkness. It is the underground perspective that gives us entry to the realm of the dead, and we need these shades to give us body, and paradoxically perhaps, to bring us life. But in alchemical terms, and for the Sufi mystics, the depths and the heights are the same. The roots in the earth and the branches in Heaven ultimately meet. Corbin knows that every being has a Dark Face and a Light Face. He would strongly caution that you have to distinguish among kinds of Darkness and he surely would refuse to travel many of the paths Hillman does. But in seeking that light and heat the animates everything, the source of which is that archetypal power and enthusiasm, Hillman's Hades and the Heavens of Corbin are conjoined.

Trying to come to terms with the differences between Hillman and Corbin has occupied me for a long time. They do not have an easy marriage. In some respects they have a great deal in common – in others they are radically opposed. Sometimes I think it makes sense to say that they are doing very different things in the same way. The one is a postmodern pagan American psychotherapist and culture critic. The other an eclectic, prodigious French scholar and mystical theologian, a heretic on the margins of the grand

---

18 Ibid., 131-32.

tradition of the great monotheisms. They moved in very different worlds. What they share however is profoundly important: a passionate belief in the utterly central place of imagination in the fabric of reality and a commitment to the importance of the freedom of the individual human soul. One reason perhaps that they have engaged me for so long is that I need to understand the ways of imagination and what can come out of it. Sonu Shamdasani, the historian, Jung scholar, and editor of the *Red Book,* has said that after a descent into the dark chaos of the imagination, Jung established a psychology; William Blake, a great art; and Emmanuel Swedenborg, a prophetic religion. Clearly, many things can come of that descent. Henry Corbin believed that all the symbols of religion come to us from the imaginal world. For Hillman, following Jung and Corbin, we are always in psyche; psyche is image, and images are the living body of the imaginal world. I feel this very strongly. We are in the belly of the beast all the time, riding the great wave, living on the edge of chaos, feeling that archetypal rush of enthusiasm for life, the heat of the flame of things just under the surface all the time, and sometimes blazing forth. How we are to best manage this fate depends on how we understand and relate to imagination as it manifests in us everyday. I think Hillman and Corbin each provide considerable guidance, but their styles differ a great deal – and in those very differences I have hoped to find clues that may help us each make spaces and find our own ways of coping, and not follow blindly in the paths of others.

Coda: The Poetic Basis of the Mind

I want to close with a couple of quotes from Henri Cartier-Bresson, the great twentieth-century French photorapher. He was well known for his astonishing photos of course, and also for the idea of the "decisive moment." He once said "Photography is not like painting. There is a creative fraction of a second when you are taking a picture. Your eye must see a composition or an expression that life itself offers you, and you must know with intuition when to click the camera. That is the moment the photographer is creative. Oop! The Moment! Once you miss it, it is gone forever."[19] I think that a certain approach to photography can in fact heighten our awareness of the life in things, of the beauty in the simplest objects, the most commonplace events. We all need some practice or better, practices, that help us cultivate this kind of seeing or sensing. We must do anything we can to help us be in the world, to love the world with all our heart, all our senses. In a 1971 interview, Cartier-Bresson spoke about photography, but I think his words help bring to life some of what I have been trying to get at with this book:

> Poetry is the essence of everything, and it's through deep contact with reality and living fully that you reach poetry. Very often I see photographers cultivating the strangeness or awkwardness of a scene, thinking it is poetry. No. Poetry is two elements which are suddenly in conflict—a spark between two elements. But it's given very seldom, and you

---

19 Adam Bernstein, "The Acknowledged Master of the Moment," http://www.washingtonpost.com/wp-dyn/articles/A39981-2004Aug4.html (accessed 2/15/2015).

can't look for it. It's like if you look for inspiration. No, it just comes by enriching yourself and living. You have to forget yourself. You have to be yourself and you have to forget yourself so that the image comes much stronger—what you want by getting involved completely in what you are doing and not thinking. Ideas are very dangerous. You must think all the time, but when you photograph, you aren't trying to push a point or prove something. You don't prove anything. It comes by itself... But as for me, I enjoy shooting a picture. Being present. It's a way of saying, "Yes! Yes! Yes!" It's like the last three words of Joyce's *Ulysses,* which is one of the most tremendous works which have ever been written. It's "Yes, yes, yes." And photography is like that. It's yes, yes, yes. And there are no maybes. All the maybes should go to the trash, because it's an instant, it's a moment, it's there! And it's respect of it and tremendous enjoyment to say, "Yes!" Even if it's something you hate. Yes! It's an affirmation.[20]

20   Sheila Turner-Seed, "Henri Cartier-Bresson: 'There Are No Maybes,'" http://lens.blogs.nytimes.com/2013/06/21/cartier-bres-son-there-are-no-maybes/ (accessed 2/15/2015).

Praise for Imaginal Love

Imaginal Love is a work of vital imagination, at once personal, formally audacious, penetrating, and richly insightful. Beginning with the premise of the inherent and initiatic complexity of Henry Corbin's thought, and building on the intricately laid foundation of the four previous volumes in his Corbin Quartet, Tom Cheetham brings his considerable learning and experience to bear on a dynamic, psycho-cosmological reading of Corbin's mighty influence on the work of archetypal psychologist James Hillman, and those modern and contemporary poets, including Robert Duncan and Charles Olson, some of whose works have been guided significantly by Hillman's ideas. For anyone interested in the overlapping open fields of depth psychology and Projective Verse, *Imaginal Love* is essential.
– Peter O'Leary, poet and author of *The Phosphorescence of Thought* and *Gnostic Contagion: Robert Duncan and the Poetry of Illness*

Cheetham's book is a jewel that returns us to the "wild energies of creation" through his lucid and passionate dedication to the necessity of imagination for soul. His book offers the essence of these thinkers as alchemical transformers of being in the *anima mundi*. *Imaginal Love* returns psyche to cosmos: as organ of imag(e)ining where we embody the angels.
– Susan Rowland, author of *Jung as a Writer* and *The Eco-critical Psyche: Literature, Evolution, Complexity and Jung*

Tom Cheetham shows the heights that independent scholars outside academia can achieve. His prior work has virtually defined independent scholarship on Henry Corbin. In *Imaginal Love,* he has turned his gifts to "the meanings of imagination in James Hillman and Henry Corbin." The result is a powerful contribution to our understanding of the full meaning of imaginal love – and the central role of such love in human life.
– Michael Lerner, President & Cofounder, Commonweal

I will not forget this book. It has subtly but, I suspect, permanently shifted the way I look at reality, the way I listen to language.
– Cynthia Bourgeault, retreat leader and author of *The Wisdom Way of Knowing, The Holy Trinity and the Law of Three,* and *Mystical Hope*